Teaching Middle School Students to Be Active Researchers

Judith M. Zorfass

with Harriet Copel

Association for Supervision and Curriculum Development
Alexandria, Virginia USA

Association for Supervision and Curriculum Development
1703 N. Beauregard St. • Alexandria, VA 22311-1714 USA
Telephone: 1-800-933-2723 or 703-578-9600
Web site: http://www.ascd.org • E-mail: member@ascd.org

Gene R. Carter, *Executive Director*
Michelle Terry, *Associate Executive Director*, Program Development
Nancy Modrak, *Director, Publishing*
John O'Neil, *Acquisitions Director*
Mark Goldberg, *Development Editor*
Julie Houtz, *Managing Editor of Books*
Carolyn R. Pool, *Associate Editor*
Charles D. Halverson, *Project Assistant*
Gary Bloom, *Director, Design and Production Services*
Karen Monaco, *Senior Designer*
Tracey A. Smith, *Production Manager*
Dina Murray, *Production Coordinator*
John Franklin, *Production Coordinator*
Valerie Sprague, *Desktop Publisher*

Printed in the United States of America.

s11/98

ASCD Stock No.: 198180
ASCD member price: $15.95   nonmember price: $18.95

Library of Congress Cataloging-in-Publication Data
Zorfass, Judith M., 1944-
    Teaching middle school students to be active researchers /
Judith M. Zorfass with Harriet Copel.
       p. cm.
    Includes bibliographical references.
    ISBN 0-87120-304-91 (pbk.)
    1. Middle school teaching—United States. 2. Research—Study and
teaching (Middle school)—United States. 3. Information
retrieval—Study and teaching (Middle school)—United States. 4.
Interdisciplinary approach in education—United States. 5. Active
learning—United States. I. Copel, Harriet, 1949- II. Association
for Supervision and Curriculum Development. III. Title.
LB1623 .Z67 1998
373.1102—ddc21
                                                    98-40096
                                                    CIP

03 02 01 00 99 98   10 9 8 7 6 5 4 3 2 1

Teaching Middle School Students to Be Active Researchers

Figures

Preface

This book draws on my experiences as the director of projects and initiatives spanning more than a decade of work at Education Development Center, Inc. (EDC) in Newton, Massachusetts. In 1986, the U.S. Department of Education, Office of Special Education Projects (OSEP), funded EDC to study what it takes to effectively integrate technology into the middle school curriculum so as to benefit students both with and without learning disabilities. This three-year effort was a partnership between EDC and Technical Education Research Centers (TERC). After working in four suburban, rural, and urban middle schools, we concluded that technology-driven reform cannot achieve its desired results *unless it is carefully tied to a strong middle school curriculum that meets the needs of young adolescents.*

Research Projects in Middle School

We also found that a common middle school rite of passage was carrying out a research project. Often, however, this research project fell short of what teachers, students, and parents envisioned as its goals. Instead of teaching students how to become active researchers who developed lifelong learning skills, research became a mechanical chore that was most often completed in a frantic rush the night before a report was due. At that time, we became aware of Ken Macrorie's book (1988), *The I-Search Paper.*

The I-Search concept had a powerful mix of ingredients (e.g., respecting curiosity, supporting independence, fostering creativity, balancing action and reflection) that we believed would capture the imaginations of both middle school teachers and their students. In the I-Search process, we saw an opportunity to deepen and enrich existing research projects in three ways. First, the I-Search approach could make research more learner centered and less teacher directed. Second, the approach could encourage students with diverse needs to work together as collaborators. Third, the I-Search approach could provide a natural context for using technology, media, and a variety of materials.

A Practical Guide

To provide teachers with a practical guide for designing and implementing I-Search Units, EDC developed, piloted, and published the first version of the Make It Happen! approach in 1991. Make It Happen! included a facilitator's guide, teachers' materials (*The Teacher's Guide to Designing an I-Search Unit*), and videos. EDC piloted the approach in four middle schools in Massachusetts, New Hampshire, and New York (Lawrence Middle School, which is featured in this book). The middle school in New Hampshire was featured in a chapter of the 1992 *ASCD Curriculum Handbook* (Zorfass, Morocco, & Lory, 1991).

To examine the impact of I-Search Units on teachers and students, we carried out a study at the John Glenn Middle School in Bedford, Massachusetts, and the Crispus Attucks Middle School in Indianapolis, Indiana. We feature the teachers and students from both schools in this book. For this project, we developed the *Search Organizer* software (1996) to guide students through the I-Search Unit. We also revised Make It Happen! (1996) by expanding some sections and materials and streamlining others. The newer version shows how interdisciplinary curriculum units can and should be linked to a district's performance standards. We also created a World Wide Web site to disseminate information and give people around the country a forum in which to discuss classroom practice and problems (http://www.edc.org/FSC/MIH/).

Since 1991, when Make It Happen! first became widely available to schools, my colleagues and I at EDC, as well as a cadre of EDC consultants, began offering technical assistance to schools implementing I-Search Units. For example, we worked with many of the 16 school districts in Indiana that were part of the Middle Grades Initiative Project (MGIP), funded by the Lilly Endowment Inc., in addition to providing help to schools in Pennsylvania, Iowa, New York, New Hampshire, California, Alaska, Puerto Rico, Maryland, and Massachusetts.

The Voices in the Book

This book contains four voices. First, my contribution derives from my background as a researcher, product developer, and trainer. In all of these roles, I have worked closely with teachers and students to develop and refine I-Search Units—and then to study their use in actual practice.

The second voice belongs to Harriet Copel, who tirelessly worked with me to prepare this book. Her valuable perspective stems from many sources. When we piloted the earliest version of Make It Happen! in Lawrence, Harriet was the district's technology specialist. After the pilot, she continued to work with her teachers in her new role as assistant principal. Over time, all three of the school's 7th grade teams implemented I-Search Units with Harriet's facilitation (Zorfass & Copel, 1995). Recently, she carried the approach with her when she became principal of the Mattlin Middle School in Plainview, New York. Harriet is also one of EDC's leading consultants, having provided training to teams in Indiana, Iowa, and New York.

Third are the voices of my EDC colleagues and the outside consultants who not only helped to develop, pilot, produce, and publish Make It Happen! but who have also provided technical assistance to schools across the country. In particular, without the work of Catherine Morocco, Arlene Remz, Shira Persky, Barbara Zeno, Paul Giguere, Carol Howard, Nina-Olff Paul, Mary-Pat Hatcher-Disler, Francene Donahue, and Cynthia

Warger, no 10-year effort would have been possible.

Most important are the voices of middle school teachers and students. Given that over the past 10 years we have carried out research, in addition to providing technical assistance, a natural part of the documentation process has involved conducting interviews, writing field notes of classroom observations, and gathering mounds of student and teacher work. Extracting from this rich database, I have tried, whenever possible, to use the actual spoken and written words of the teachers and students who willingly gave their time and energy.

Acknowledgments

I am blessed to have so many colleagues at EDC who generated ideas, reviewed drafts, offered encouragement, and helped me carve out time for writing. In particular, my deep-felt appreciation goes to Nancy Ames, who, as a "critical" friend, is my best friend because she always pairs a critical comment with an excellent suggestion. Lori DiGisi, Anne Shure, Carolyn Wyatt, and Arlene Remz were excellent reviewers who told me, as sensitively as they knew how, what I needed to hear to strengthen the book. Carrie Campbell and Bonnie Johnson deserve praise and thanks for preparing the manuscript and figures. Outside of EDC, my husband Paul, my daughters Lauren and Deborah (who edited my work), sons-in-law, and granddaughter Hannah provided huge doses of support.

Introduction

The parallels between the development of babies from birth to age 1 and of young adolescents from 10 to 14 years of age are intriguing. I am fascinated by the similarities between Hannah, my first grandchild, who is midway through her first year of life, and the young adolescents I see when visiting middle schools across the country. Both are simultaneously undergoing rapid changes on many levels. Week by week, I am thrilled to note how Hannah's looks have changed, how she's found new ways to interact with her world, and how she is more vocal and expressive in her communications. I am just as intrigued by the changing appearance, beliefs, and behavior of young adolescents as they undergo their own physical, cognitive, social, and emotional metamorphoses.

The second similarity is the need for both babies and young adolescents to understand their worlds through exploration. I see Hannah investigating her world through watching, touching, tasting, and listening. Much more sophisticated, young adolescents read, watch television, log onto the Internet, make telephone calls, and travel to new locations that are still close to home (alas, many of these trips are to the shopping mall). Right now, it's easy for Hannah's "teachers"—her parents, extended family, and friends—to provide her with the perfect mix of stimulation and nurturing she needs to make meaning of her world. But what about young adolescents? What mix is needed to help them capitalize on their natural curiosity, investigative powers, social acumen, and expanding cognitive abilities? How do their many teachers help them to be active learners who, just like Hannah, seek to understand their world?

Purpose of This Book

This book describes in detail one specific way middle school educators can meet their young adolescents' needs to be active learners. The vehicle is the I-Search Curriculum Unit, based on Ken Macrorie's book *The I-Search Paper* (1988). In a carefully planned I-Search Unit, teachers employ solid instructional practices to help students carry out four basic elements of active research:

- Pose questions after becoming immersed in compelling information.
- Learn how to access varied resources and materials.
- Make meaning from the information they have gathered.
- Represent their knowledge in varied formats.

This book is written for the hundreds of thousands of middle school teachers, administrators, specialists, and other staff throughout the country who want to know how to teach students how to conduct meaningful research. These practitioners are professionally and personally excited by the challenges they face in teaching young adolescents. Daily, they strive to meet the developmental needs of students who are ready to assume more control over their own learning, eager to explore new environments, stimulated by a variety of resources, and motivated to collaborate with their peers. Many teachers long for clear models, concrete images, and specific suggestions to answer questions like these:

• What does the instructional process look like when it's working well?

• What are realistic expectations for students?

• How will I know if they, and I, are succeeding?

This book meets this compelling need. It delineates the I-Search model, presenting powerful, in-depth images of practice. It focuses on the relationships among teaching, learning, and assessment. It presents clear and vivid examples of teaching practices in diverse classroom settings, as well as abundant examples of students' work to reveal how individual students are constructing knowledge over time. Last, it integrates a theoretical discussion of brain-based learning, cognitive and moral development, and multiple intelligence.

An added strength of the book is its attention to standards-based education, a rallying point for today's educational initiatives. Throughout, examples show how teachers can take advantage of standards, particularly in English language arts, science, and social studies, to guide and buttress their ongoing curriculum efforts.

Structure of the Book

This book has six chapters. The first chapter defines active research, explains how the four phases of an I-Search Unit are designed to promote active research, discusses why it is developmentally appropriate and important for young adolescents to be active researchers, and presents evidence showing that active research produces positive results. Each of the next four chapters focuses on a successive phase of the I-Search Unit. Chapter 2 describes how teachers guide students to pose I-Search questions after becoming immersed in activities related to an interdisciplinary theme. Chapter 3 shows how teachers help students learn how to access a variety of materials. Chapter 4 focuses on ways teachers help students integrate and process the information they have gathered. Chapter 5 illustrates ways in which teachers help students represent their knowledge in written papers and through exhibitions. The final chapter describes what it takes, in terms of facilitation and organizational support, to successfully design, implement, and reflect on I-Search Units. The appendix includes 10 sections describing planning and assessment criteria, from planning immersion activities, to creating guidelines for student peer conferences, to developing rubrics for assessment, to evaluating the implementation of an I-Search Unit.

Defining Active Research

Scene 1: Returning to school after collecting water samples from a nearby stream, the 8th graders test the water for bacteria. After charting the results, they write reflections in their journals. One student writes, "I'm surprised to see the high level of bacteria in the water. How could this hurt us? When we learned about waterborne diseases in Mexico during Spanish class, I thought that was a distant problem. Could something like this happen close to home?"

Scene 2: Seventh graders tumble off the school bus and head toward the university library. Librarians, having been prepped by the middle school teachers, await the students inside. Each student, armed with a research question about some aspect of natural disasters, is about to begin browsing through materials and resources. The students' mission is to develop a research plan that includes books, magazines, newspapers, videos,

names of people to interview, and places to visit.

Scene 3: Jackie, a middle school student, sits at her computer. Index cards containing notes about the factors contributing to breast cancer are scattered nearby. On the screen are three columns: social factors, biological factors, and psychological factors. After reviewing each card, she types the relevant information under the appropriate heading.

Scene 4: The lights dim, the audience of family and friends hushes, and the curtain rises on the auditorium stage. Three 6th graders, in costume, enter from the left. They are presenting information they gathered about the Middle Ages. One recites an original poem, another displays a mural, and the third reads a biographical sketch. Later, the audience will have a chance to read papers written by all the students and view various exhibitions.

What Is Active Research?

What do these scenarios depicting middle school students all have in common? The answer is that they are all examples of active research. Active researchers are meaning makers. They are self-motivated inquirers, investigators, and seekers of knowledge. Each active researcher has a thirst for knowledge, a need to know, a desire to learn, or as Macrorie (1988) puts it, "a genuine itch" that needs to be scratched "until you've quieted it" (p. 100).

Each of the scenarios illustrates a different facet of active research.

• In Scene 1, students are provoked by what they are learning and want to learn more. By becoming immersed in ideas, students begin to pose questions or problems that drive the inquiry process. The questions or problems focus on content—but are also driven by social concerns or personally meaningful issues.

• In Scene 2, students develop a plan of action to guide their investigations. The plan draws on many sources of information and can change over time as new and unexpected doors to information appear and open.

• In Scene 3, students not only gather information from a variety of resources but also consciously organize and make meaning of this information. Constructing knowledge involves analysis and synthesis; these processes involve critical thinking.

• In Scene 4, using varied media, students express and display what they have learned to an audience. The inquiry process deepens the researchers' understanding of an issue or question and strengthens their skills as independent learners. In addition, by sharing information, students contribute to the knowledge base of others.

Carrying out active research is not a one-time experience. The active researcher does not engage in inquiry for a prescribed period of time and then stop. Instead, a search for knowledge raises new questions and identifies other areas to explore. The active researcher also reflects on the process of research so that he or she can be a more effective researcher in the future. By reflecting, researchers come to recognize the iterative nature of the process, the ways in which it requires collaboration with others, and the learner's own best strategies for making meaning.

In this book, we delineate how teachers across the United States have helped middle school students become active researchers at a developmentally appropriate and critical point in their lives.

Why Is Active Research Developmentally Appropriate for Middle Schoolers?

Whenever I discuss active research with middle school teachers, we always start off with an exercise to anchor the conversation. We close our eyes, imagine just one student, and identify a characteristic that vividly captures that young adolescent's developmental needs. Whether we do this exercise in the North, South, East, or West; in urban, suburban, or rural schools; or in low, middle, or high socioeconomic areas, teachers respond in much the same ways. Here are the kinds of remarks that teachers make about young adolescents:

- They can't sit still for long; they need to be moving and doing all the time.
- Peer acceptance is critical; being part of the group means everything.
- They're curious and inquisitive; they want to know more about people, places, and how and why things work.
- They are capable of thinking. Although sometimes their thinking is more concrete and at other times more abstract, they are able to reason, contemplate, and think critically.
- They are yearning to discover who they are and what they are capable of doing, especially as they move away from the security of the family.
- They demonstrate caring and concern for others, have a growing sense of justice, and seek clarity about what is right and what is wrong.
- They desire some structure and organization, even while they may act as if they are resisting it.
- Each one wants to show what he or she is capable of creating and accomplishing.

In addition, teachers usually mention middle schoolers' uneven growth spurts—given the rapid physical, cognitive, moral, and psychosocial changes of 10–14-year-olds. For example, teachers note differences in cognitive development. They discuss how some students are literal and concrete, focusing more on classification or relating parts to the whole. Others, meanwhile, are capable of dealing with abstractions, reasoning about the future, and developing and testing hypotheses. Waxing philosophical, someone usually concludes that these are the challenges and joys of working with this age group, which, of course, elicits chuckles mingled with groans.

Teachers' astute observations are borne out by recent research. Over the past 25 years, researchers have begun to recognize early adolescence as a formative period of development that is unique and distinct from late childhood and later adolescence or adulthood (Ames & Miller, 1994; Urdan, Klein, & Medrich, 1997). Drawing on Manning's (1993) excellent synthesis, I summarize key findings about the characteristics of young adolescents. For example, in terms of physical development, they experience a growth spurt marked by a rapid increase in body size, as well as readily apparent skeletal and structural changes. In terms of psychosocial development, they shift their allegiance and affiliation from parents and teachers toward the peer group, which becomes the prime source for standards and models of behavior. Cognitive development is characterized by an increasing ability to think abstractly, reflectively, critically, and hypothetically, while making reasoned moral and ethical choices.

As a group, we, the teachers, then discuss the developmental appropriateness of active research for young adolescents. For example, it capitalizes on their innate curiosity to explore topics of importance both to them and their community. Use of varied materials and resources meets their need to be fully engaged learners. Active research can be a collaborative effort that builds on the young adolescent's need to be constructively involved with peers (Slavin, 1990). Finally, the process meets their need to find creative outlets to represent knowledge.

As this discussion proceeds, teachers exclaim, "OK. I'm convinced!" Then, they ask, "Tell me how to bring active research into my classroom?

How can we work together as interdisciplinary teams?" This is my segue to present the I-Search Unit, one type of interdisciplinary curriculum unit that promotes active research.

How Does the I-Search Unit Promote Active Research?

Ken Macrorie first coined the term "I-Search" in *The I-Search Paper* (1988). For Macrorie, I-Searchers go "on an adventure, an odyssey, that eventually brings them home . . . and then they tell the story of the trip, as Homer's hero did" (p.100). Others have seen the power of the I-Search; teachers have used it in elementary through high school settings (Joyce & Tallman, 1997; Kaszyca & Krueger, 1994; Morocco & Nelson, 1990). In fact, Nancy Lory, at Keene State College in New Hampshire, requires that her undergraduate education majors carry out an I-Search to pursue an education-related topic.

In our work with teachers, our goal was to promote active research in today's middle schools, where interdisciplinary instruction was becoming more prevalent. Therefore, we expanded on Macrorie's work in two ways. First, we introduced the idea of students carrying out their search around big ideas that spanned the disciplines. Second, we made the research process explicit by identifying four phases of instruction.

Conducting Research Around Big Ideas

In our version of I-Search, the unit is interdisciplinary, organized around a central theme.

Heidi Jacobs (1989) defines interdisciplinary curriculum as "a knowledge view and curriculum approach that consciously applies methodology and language from more than one discipline to examine a central theme, issue, problem, topic, or experience" (p. 8). She recommends that each interdisciplinary unit have an organizing center that "should neither be so general and all-encompassing that it is beyond the scope of a definitive investigation, nor . . . be so narrow that it restricts the parameters of study" (p. 54).

Perkins and Blythe (1994) believe that a good theme must be generative. It is central to the discipline, accessible to students, and connects to diverse topics. Beane (1990) suggests that the organizing center of a thematic unit should be drawn from the intersecting concerns of early adolescence and issues in the larger world. For example, a curriculum theme such as "interdependence" connects the social concern of global interdependence with a young adolescent's concern about finding a place within a group. Other strong themes that make this connection are transitions, identities, social structures, independence, conflict resolution, commercialism, justice, caring, and institutions (Beane, 1990).

In an I-Search Unit, we want students to make conceptual links across disciplines so that knowledge is integrated, not fragmented. Our guiding philosophy is that less is more; it is better for students to develop deep and thorough understandings of core concepts than to superficially cover a vast number of often unrelated concepts. This mirrors the philosophy of the national standards, where each of the major disciplines has identified big, important ideas that organize curriculums across the grades. For example, Figure 1.1 presents the big ideas that organize science content across the grades, according to the National Research Council (1996).

The teachers we have worked with find that the strongest interdisciplinary themes:

- Deal with important ideas that are linked to national standards, curriculum frameworks, or local standards adopted by the district or school.
- Link content across disciplines in a meaningful way.
- Are socially meaningful.
- Allow students to develop skills in a meaningful context.
- Are motivating to students and relevant to their lives and experiences.
- Are motivating to teachers.
- Generate interesting issues and questions that students will want to explore.
- Allow exploration through varied materials and media.
- Have resources and materials that are available and accessible.

Some examples of actual themes chosen by teachers, often with input from students, tend to fall under the following categories:

- The environment (e.g., pollution; Native Americans as environmentalists; rivers).
- Natural phenomena (e.g., the human body; natural disasters; nature's unsolved mysteries).
- Technology (e.g., inventions; communicating through technology).
- Major historical events such as wars (e.g., the two fronts of World War II).
- Human endeavor (e.g., careers for the 21st century; social unrest).
- Migration and immigration (e.g., Westward Ho!; Coming to America; California, Here I Come!).

FIGURE 1.1
Major Themes in Science Standards (Grades 5–8)

- *Physical Science:* Properties and changes in properties in matter, motion and forces, transfer of energy.
- *Life Science:* Structure and function in living systems, reproduction and heredity, regulation and behavior, populations and ecosystems, diversity and adaptations of organisms.
- *Earth and Space Science:* Structure of the Earth's system, Earth's history, Earth in the solar system.
- *Science and Technology:* Abilities of technological design, understandings about science and technology.
- *Science in Personal and Social Perspectives:* Personal health; populations, resources, and environments; natural hazards; risks and benefits; science and technology in society.
- *History and Nature of Science:* Science as a human endeavor, nature of science, history of science.

Source: National Research Council. (1996). *National Science Education Standards.* Washington, DC: National Academy Press.

The unit's theme is clarified and elaborated on with three or four big ideas or "overarching concepts." Regarding the "less is more" approach, the overarching concepts represent the conceptual underpinnings of the unit. Important to know about, they are relevant to the world and capable of evoking an emotional response. Drawing on the construct of essential questions and essential understanding in the work of the ATLAS Communities Project (Orrell, 1996), overarching concepts have three main characteristics. First, they are focused and relate directly to the heart of the theme. Second, they elaborate the theme by representing the key, basic ideas related to the content surrounding the theme. Third, they require students to consider multiple perspectives related to the theme and to analyze and make judgments about information. Figure 1.2 presents a typical "thematic web" with the theme of technology at the center and the overarching concepts radiating outward. It was developed in Lawrence, New York, by a 7th grade team with Harriet Copel's help.

In an I-Search Unit, the theme and concepts become the framework for inquiry. Every student in the class (or team, or group) is engaged in a personal search related to the theme and overarching concepts. This creates communities of learners involved in seeking answers to similar, but not identical, questions (Brooks & Brooks, 1993). If the theme is generative, then every student should be able to find something relevant to investigate. Interesting themes such as "change" or "patterns in our environment" might translate into great interdisciplinary units, but not necessarily great I-Search Units. Because they are abstractions, it can be difficult for students to pose clear, researchable questions that use varied resources.

Making Research Explicit

We want our young adolescents to develop inquiry skills so that they can be active researchers both now and in the future. This goal is being touted in the national standards in English language arts, science, social studies, and mathematics. Figure 1.3 (on p. 8) lists specific standards excerpted from these four disciplines.

An I-Search Unit involves a process for generating a question, developing a search plan, gathering and integrating information, and representing what has been learned to others. Expanding on Macrorie's work, we define four phases of instruction, as shown in Figure 1.4 (on p. 9). A unit, carried out by two or more teachers, usually lasts between 8 and 12 weeks.

Phase I. In Phase I, teachers from different disciplines work together to actively engage students in a variety of authentic activities. Within these activities, teachers elicit students' prior knowledge, help students build background knowledge, have students reflect on what they are learning, and help them find questions to pursue. As a bonus, these varied immersion activities model for students the multiple ways to gather information. Chapter 2 shows the thoughtful and effective ways teachers help students become immersed and pose individual questions.

Phase II. In this phase, teachers guide each student to develop a search plan. The plan has two components: specifying what varied materials and resources students will use, and in what order or sequence they will do so. Teachers set criteria so that students do four things:

• *Read* books, magazines, newspapers, and reference materials (both in print and on CD-ROMs and the Internet).

• *Watch* videos and television documentaries.

• *Ask* people for information through interviews and surveys.

• *Do* something active, such as carrying out an experiment, doing a computer simulation, or going on a field trip.

Chapter 3 provides an in-depth view of how teachers ensure, before and throughout the unit, that students will use these varied materials and resources.

Phase III. After they develop their plans, students gather, sort, and integrate information. In this sustained period of time, students analyze and synthesize information to make meaning. Teachers use a variety of strategies to support students as they delve into content, form

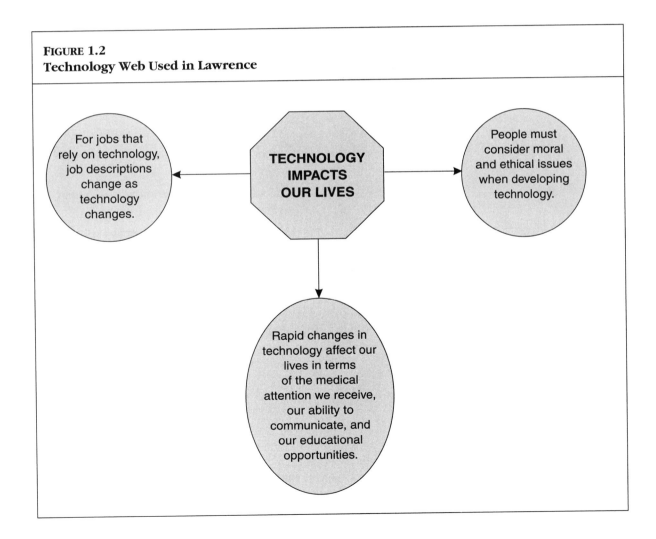

FIGURE 1.2
Technology Web Used in Lawrence

FIGURE 1.3
Inquiry-Based Performance Standards

Discipline and Source	Performance: Focus on Inquiry
English Language Arts National Council of Teachers of English and International Reading Association, 1996.	"Students conduct research on issues and interests by generating ideas and questions, and by posing problems. They gather, evaluate, and synthesize data from a variety of sources (e.g., print and non-print text, artifacts, people) to communicate their discoveries in ways that suit their purpose and audience." "Students use a variety of technological and information resources (e.g., libraries, databases, computer networks, videos) to gather and synthesize information and to create and communicate knowledge."
Science National Research Council, 1996.	"The inquiry process in science involves students in: • identifying questions that can be answered through scientific investigations • designing and conducting a scientific investigation • using appropriate tools and techniques to gather, analyze, and interpret data • developing descriptions, explanations, predictions, and models using evidence • thinking critically and logically to make the relationships between evidence and explanations"
Social Studies National Council for the Social Studies, 1994.	In social studies, it "is important that students become able to connect knowledge, skills, and values to civic action as they engage in social inquiry." Two of the key skills are acquiring information and manipulating data, and developing and presenting policies, arguments, and stories.
Mathematics The National Council of Teachers of Mathematics, 1989.	"Mathematical power includes the ability to explore, conjecture, and reason logically; to solve non-routine problems; to communicate about and through mathematics; and to connect ideas within mathematics and between mathematics and other intellectual activity. Mathematical power also involves . . . a disposition to seek, evaluate, and use quantitative and spatial information in solving problems and making decisions."

FIGURE 1.4
I-Search Process: Four Instructional Phases

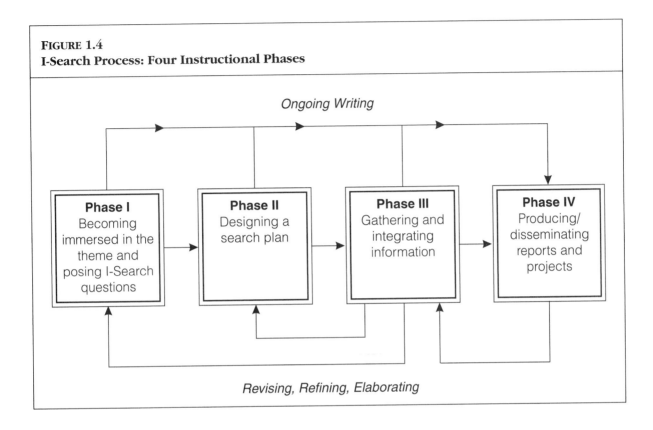

conceptualizations and gestalts (Caine & Caine, 1991), and think critically about what they are learning. Chapter 4 depicts the meaning-making process by students in diverse settings.

Phase IV. In this phase, teachers give students time, a method, and supports to produce a written paper or prepare an exhibition that will represent what they have learned. Students engage in the process of designing, drafting, revising, editing, and producing or publishing their work using multimedia presentations, videos, skits, posters, experiments, or a performing art form. Whatever format they choose, teachers want students to convey information about the following: My Search Question, My Search Process, What I Have Learned, What This Means to Me, and References (see Macrorie, 1988). Chapter

5 shows how teachers set criteria and help students represent knowledge.

How Do Teachers Promote Successful, Active Researchers?

Teachers work hard to design and implement their I-Search Units. Their challenge is to design supportive structures so that every student will be a successful active researcher who is both a learner and a contributor. During a period of time designated for curriculum design (see description in Chapter 6), teachers determine the theme and overarching concepts for the unit; they design activities for each of the four phases of instruction, they determine what they will collect as evidence of student learning, and they set criteria for products. Each one of their decisions is aimed at creating an opportunity for students to make choices as active researchers. Students can choose their search question, determine what materials and resources they will use, select strategies for analyzing and comprehending information, and determine how best to represent their knowledge.

Throughout implementation of each phase of the unit, teachers unfailingly provide students with support. Teachers take to heart these five design principles: They are clear about and articulate the goals of active research; use developmentally appropriate practices; thoughtfully use brain-based instructional strategies; set expectations for students to use varied materials and resources, and model how to do so; and engage in ongoing assessment so that they can intervene when needed to ensure success.

Teachers Are Clear About and Articulate Goals

Teachers are clear that there are four sets of goals. First, they want students to understand that the I-Search is an inquiry process and that, by carrying it out, the students will develop skills to be active researchers. Teachers often say to students: "We want you to *acquire the skills* needed to be active researchers. And we want you to *reflect* on what you are doing so you can understand the process. And we want you to *figure out what you learned* from this experience that you can carry with you into the future."

This leads us to the second goal. Teachers are clear that the search process is not just a

process for the sake of being a process. Therefore, they explain to their students that the goal of carrying out the I-Search process is to acquire worthwhile knowledge. They say, "By applying the search process, you will learn something." They want students to understand that the process and the product are inextricably interwoven.

The third goal centers on psychosocial skills. Teachers want students to become both independent learners and effective collaborators. As independent learners, students are self-regulated, self-disciplined, and self-directed. They are able to formulate and carry out realistic plans, be aware of their own thinking, seek out and use feedback, and evaluate the effectiveness of their own actions to make needed modifications. As collaborators, teachers want students to both contribute to and personally benefit from group participation. Within groups, students listen to each other with respect, build on one another's ideas, assist each other in drawing implications, and help the group meet shared goals. These goals are also visible in the national standards, often under the heading of lifelong learning standards (Marzano et al., 1993).

This brings us to the fourth goal, enhancing students' self-respect and self-knowledge. Teachers believe that by constructing knowledge, developing and applying skills, learning how to work independently, and becoming collaborators, students will develop a genuine sense of self-respect and self-esteem—a notable by-product of applying effort—and come to believe in their own powers as learners and thinkers. As two students from Boston relate:

> I appreciate myself as a researcher and a writer because I was successful. I am intelligent, independent, and responsible enough to do work on my own without people on me 24 [hours a day] 7 [days a week] to telling me what to do, when to do it, and how to do it.
>
> When I want to do it, I know I can. I really learned a lot . . . . Once in a while I enjoy being smart.

The four goals are not just for academically talented or able students. They apply as well for students who are considered to be at risk for school failure, have disabilities that create barriers for learning, or who come to middle school with a first language other than English. In fact, the two preceding quotes are from students who would typically be considered at risk. It is important for students at risk to become motivated learners who expand their knowledge, learn the kinds of skills and processes they can apply in other contexts, improve their psychosocial skills, and develop a sense of self-worth.

Teachers Use Developmentally Appropriate Practices

In designing and implementing an I-Search Unit, teachers do not lose sight of the developmental needs of young adolescents. What is the point of our knowing that young adolescents are fidgety and require movement if we then plan instruction that keeps them seat bound and passive? What is the value of our knowing how critical communication is with peers, if we keep them as solitary workers who have no opportunity to collaborate? Figure 1.5 (see p. 13) shows how specific instructional practices respond to the developmental needs of young adolescents.

Teachers Use Brain-Based Instructional Strategies

Researchers such as Caine and Caine (1991) and Sylwester (1995) are contributing to a growing knowledge base about how children learn and what promotes learning (see "How Children Learn," the March 1997 issue of *Educational Leadership*). We are coming to understand and appreciate how the human brain is designed to seek out, perceive, and understand patterns. To understand our world, our brains create patterns by organizing and categorizing experience. Prior knowledge becomes the foundation for relating seemingly random pieces of information to one another. Over a period of time, as learners fit information together in a meaningful way, they develop a *gestalt:* a coherent understanding that becomes a natural and integrated part of what the learner knows and does in the present and future. The patterns we form make sense to us because they are influenced by our cognitive abilities, emotions, personal biases and prejudices, level of self-esteem, and ways we interact socially (Caine & Caine, 1991).

In a recent book, *Education on the Edge of Possibility,* Caine and Caine (1997, p. 19) present a succinct list of 12 brain/mind learning principles, as follows:

1. The brain is a complex adaptive system.

2. The brain is a social brain.

3. The search for meaning is innate.

4. The search for meaning occurs through "patterning."

5. Emotions are critical to patterning.

6. Every brain simultaneously perceives and creates parts and wholes.

7. Learning involves both focused attention and peripheral perception.

8. Learning always involves conscious and unconscious processes.

9. We have at least two ways of organizing memory.

10. Learning is developmental.

11. Complex learning is enhanced by challenge and inhibited by threat.

12. Every brain is uniquely organized.

What is exciting about the Caines' book is that it goes beyond theory to practice, reporting what happened when the Caines implemented their theories about learning in schools in California. The authors report findings that brain-based strategies promote student learning not only in the early elementary years but also in 8th and 9th grades. Young adolescents raised their grade point average and scored well on a standardized statewide algebra test.

Within an I-Search Unit, teachers use many instructional strategies that build on this knowledge base. For example, in Phase I, they design immersion activities that are challenging but not threatening. Understanding the role of emotion, teachers help students find search questions that students feel passionate about. In Phase III, teachers help students use different tools to create patterns. Teachers also encourage students to think critically about what they are learning from a moral and ethical perspective. Given that learning is socially mediated, teachers find ways for students to collaborate to construct knowledge. By introducing journals, teachers provide opportunities for reflection. Chapters 2–5 present many descriptions of these and other instructional strategies.

Teachers Use Varied Materials and Resources

Teachers use varied materials and resources for many reasons. One reason is to provide access to information, especially in immersion activities. Teachers want to tap into students' varied talents, abilities, and intelligences. They also want students to appreciate that information presented in different formats can provide different perspectives (e.g., what you learn from interviewing a survivor of a flood is different from what you learn by seeing video footage of raging waters). Teachers clearly explain to students why it is important to use varied materials and resources, and how to access them. Teachers set expectations so that students are clear about what they are expected to use as part of their search process.

A second reason is to help students meaningfully process information. For example, graphic organizers (Hyerle, 1996) can help students organize information as it relates to specific content. Teachers introduce technology tools, such as *Inspiration*, to help students make webs, flowcharts, and outlines. Some teachers use the *Search Organizer* software program that EDC developed because it is keyed to each of the four phases of instruction.

The third reason is to help students use many ways to represent their knowledge. In Phase IV, teachers can provide students with access to multimedia tools, video equipment, technology tools to create Web pages, and a vast supply of materials and resources needed to support the performing arts: art, drama, and music.

FIGURE 1.5
Developmentally Appropriate Practices in the I-Search Unit

Needs of Young Adolescents	Developmentally Appropriate Practices
To be active and to move around	During Phase I, the immersion activities involve moving and doing. Students are not sedentary as they *read, watch, ask,* and *do* to gather information in Phase III. In Phase IV, exhibitions allow students the freedom to express themselves through movement and activity.
To feel autonomous	Students develop their own questions, develop their own research plan, find their own ways to analyze information, and determine ways they want to represent knowledge.
To understand their world	The framework for the unit, the theme, and the overarching concepts are worthwhile, relevant, and meaningful to the students.
To satisfy curiosity	Each student's individual I-Search question builds on the student's ability to ask questions and their need to find out.
To be part of a group effort	The hunt for knowledge related to the theme and overarching concepts is a collective effort. Everyone contributes to developing a deep and shared knowledge base through their own investigation.
To have a support structure	The four phases of instruction make the research process explicit, set expectations, and create a timeline of what has to happen at specific times.
To work with peers	Cooperative learning is embedded throughout so that students can work and learn together.
To express their creativity and produce work	Students can represent knowledge using varied media.

Teachers Engage in Ongoing Assessment

Within each phase of the I-Search Unit, teachers set criteria that clearly let students know what they should be doing to carry out the research process and construct knowledge. Throughout the process, teachers gather evidence to indicate that students are working toward these goals. Teachers might rely on student conversations, entries in journals, work samples collected in portfolios, and "interim products." Each phase of the I-Search Unit has its own interim product. For Phase I, the interim product is the student's I-Search Question; for Phase II, the search plan; and for Phase III, charts, graphs, tables, or webs that show meaning making, drafting of paragraphs, and other indicators showing that students have connected ideas.

Rubrics set expectations and guide student self-evaluation. For example, as Figure 1.6 shows, the teachers in Lawrence, New York, developed a rubric for posing I-Search questions (Zorfass & Copel, 1995). The final product, a written paper or an exhibition, has its own set of assessment criteria (see Chapter 5 and Appendix A-6).

Ongoing assessment prevents students from becoming stuck at a particular phase, unable to successfully build on what they are already doing well. At the first signs of difficulty, teachers intervene, providing individualized support and assistance.

Does Active Research Produce Results?

As participants in reform initiatives, teachers, administrators, parents, board members, and students have every right to request evidence that active research works for young adolescents. One purpose of this book is to present compelling and detailed anecdotal evidence to that effect. To reinforce our own anecdotal data, we draw on evidence from three additional sources: research conducted by innovative practitioners, curriculum developers who evaluate the effectiveness of their materials and methods, and educational researchers who design and carry out rigorous research studies over time in classroom settings. All research we cite here focuses on the young adolescents in the middle grades.

• Carol Carlson, a middle school teacher in a lower-middle-income community outside of Chicago, began implementing a student-centered writing approach in 1991 with 7th and 8th graders. A total of 105 heterogeneously grouped students chose their own topics, worked collaboratively, conferred with teachers and peers, and published their work. After following the progress of these students over two years, Carlson was delighted with the scores from the California Achievement Tests. From the 7th to the 8th grades, her students' scores rose in language mechanics from 10.2 to 12.9 and in language expression from 9.4 to 12.9. These scores compared favorably with her 1990 test results. At that time, a similar group of students scored lower (10.7 in language mechanics and 9.9 in language expression; reported in Zemelman et al., 1993).

• Fred Carrigg, executive director for academic programs in Union City, New Jersey, and Gary Ramella, supervisor of computer operations in Union City, reported findings from a major curriculum overhaul. Union City, a poor urban district taken over by the state in 1989, had no

FIGURE 1.6
Criteria for I-Search Questions

| | Not Acceptable | | Acceptable | |
	Murky	Cloudy	Clear	Panoramic
Meaningful Problem	Topic is clear. Question is not formulated.	Topic is clear. Question is clear.	Topic is clear. Question is clear, personally significant, and answerable.	Topic is clear. Question is clear, personally significant, and answerable. Far-reaching statement and significant to society.
Research Resources	No examples.	Found at least two examples	1 book, 2 interviews, 4 newspaper articles, 1 CD-ROM, 1 video.	1 book, 2 interviews, 4 newspaper articles, 1 CD-ROM, 1 video, plus 7 examples: SIRS, electronic media.
Solution	Doesn't apply to the problem.	Not realistic but applies to the problem.	Applies to the problem. Involves self-solution.	Applies to the problem. Involves self and others in solution.

Source: Zorfass, J., & Copel, H. (1995). The I-Search: Guiding students toward relevant research. *Educational Leadership, 53* (1), 48–51.

choice but to revamp the curriculum. Carefully and thoughtfully, the district designed a curriculum that included, among other components, active learning, research, cooperative learning, project-based learning, and an infusion of technology for acquiring information. After four years of strenuous reform efforts, Carrigg and Ramella (1996) report that Union City's reading scores on the state standardized test for 8th graders

improved by 53.6 percent, writing scores rose by 42.9 percent, and mathematics scores increased by 29 percent. Their students, on average, have outperformed those in other urban districts in the state by 30 points (and their passing rates are approaching the state average).

• The U.S. Department of Education's National Diffusion Network (NDN) disseminates information about programs that have demonstrated their effectiveness in improving student performance. Many programs described in *Educational Programs That Work: The Catalogue of the National Diffusion Network* (Lang, 1995) used curriculums that embody the hallmarks of active research. One program, in particular, is a close cousin to the I-Search. The stated goals of Kids Interest Discovery Studies KITS (KIDS KITS) are to generate active, self-directed learning and higher levels of thinking. Teachers and the library media staff develop thematic kits (like units) containing books, filmstrips, tapes, and models. The program includes four phases of student involvement that encourage students to articulate questions, locate and use resources, organize information, and plan a presentation. Evidence of effectiveness comes from interviewing students in 14 rural to large urban school districts located in eight different states. Findings indicate that with increased use of the kits, students demonstrate (1) greater specificity, complexity, and multiplicity in their descriptions of the purpose of their learning activities; (2) more awareness and use of learning resources; (3) greater number of applications of information; and (4) a high level of interest and enthusiasm for research.

Other programs identified by the NDN, such as Creating Independence through Student-Owned Strategies (Project CRISS); Increase Performance by Activating Critical Thinking (IMPACT); and Study Skills Across the Curriculum, all teach students to apply study and information-processing skills to content areas in the middle school to actively search for information and construct meaning. All these programs have shown that students make gains in content knowledge and critical thinking skills (the same goals as those of I-Search).

• The most rigorous example of educational research comes from the work of Brown and Campione (1996). Over the years, their work in building a community of active learners through guided discovery has moved from the laboratory into classrooms, and finally into an entire school that they adopted. Their approach couples individual student responsibility for gathering information with communal sharing of knowledge. Teachers and students generate unit themes (e.g., changing populations), which are divided into approximately five subtopics (e.g., extinct, endangered, artificial, assisted, and urbanized populations). As a member of a small research group, each student takes responsibility for one or more of the five subtopics by preparing materials, becoming an expert on one part of the material, teaching it to others, and contributing questions for a class evaluation. Through this jigsaw process, the overall goal is for every student to master the entire theme.

Brown and Campione posed two research questions to evaluate their approach: Did the students learn anything? and How would we know if they did? To answer these questions with respect to 5th and 6th grade students, they used an extensive battery of pre- and post-knowledge tests, which were supplemented by interviews, portfolios, and student products. They administered the pre- and post-tests to three groups of students. The experimental group included the students who carried out the guided research during three units; the partial control group consisted of students who used guided research only for the first of the three units; and the control group included students who only read materials about the topics for all three units. Brown and Campione found that students in the research group and partial control groups performed equally well on Unit 1, where they were both treated the same as researchers. But the students in the research group clearly outperformed the partial control group and the read-only control group on Units 2 and 3. The researchers concluded that content-specific content is retained better by students who actively engaged in research. In addition, the supplemental measures (interviews and performance on application tasks) showed that the research group accumulated knowledge, had confidence in their opinions, and were able to reason on the basis of incomplete knowledge.

Final Comments

The millions of middle schoolers today will be the twentysomethings of the next millennium. Although some may still be in school working on graduate degrees or learning a skill, others may be contemplating entering the work force or working as employees on initial career paths. Although hard to visualize, they may be husbands and wives and even parents of young

children. Whatever their future role or position, they will need to be active researchers.

Becoming an active researcher during middle school can help students be more successful in the future. Posing questions, gathering information, analyzing that information, and thinking critically about worthwhile information contributes positively to young adolescents' overall development toward adulthood. In today's society, young adolescents face many complex choices that can often become more complex as they enter adulthood. Students can be better equipped to face those choices with more balance and reason, and far less instability and impulse, when teachers give them the opportunity to think, investigate, and grapple with issues in the safety of the middle school classroom (Harmin, 1994).

In the next four chapters, we take a close look at students grappling with complex issues. We will draw on experiences from middle school classrooms where teachers have developed and implemented I-Search Units. Here are some questions to keep in mind as you read: "What are the goals for students? What is the teacher's responsibility? What evidence is there that students are meeting these goals? How would this work for my students?"

Posing Questions Through Immersion

As a moviegoer, I get so involved in figuring out how a special effect was accomplished, that I lose interest in the movie. . . . I want to learn more technical terms and how computers and different types of cameras work and are used to create special effects. I also want to find out about special effects that are created through the use of gunpowder and explosions.

Passionate Research Questions

A passionate research question is the engine that drives active research. The desire to investigate something you are intrigued about is at the very core of active research. This is the feeling that overcame Ariel, the student from New York who describes her interest in special effects in the previous quote.

Although finding a passionate question should be a breeze for early adolescents—considering their natural inquisitiveness and blossoming conceptual abilities—this does not often occur. Consider what happens in many classrooms. A teacher announces that the class will embark on a research project about Asia the following week. The teacher then immediately invites everyone to pick a country to research. One by one, students make a selection. When all of the "good" countries are chosen, the slower-to-act students are left to accept, by default, the "leftover" countries. Some teachers even list the facts students are expected to "discover." When this happens, research becomes a rote activity, placing students in a position of finding predetermined answers to predetermined questions.

This approach violates the very premise of active research. It fails to help students generate a question that they care about and that begs for active research. Rather, active research is nipped in the bud for three reasons. Using the Asia example, the first reason is that the teacher does not begin with a conceptual framework that clearly states the big ideas about Asia. These might be related to Asia's geography, history, and cultures. Big ideas, like Sizer's (1992) essential questions, can provide the grounding for an investigation and also become the springboard for a student's individual search. Second, at this beginning stage, when content knowledge is shallow, students need to go further before they know where to dive into content. Third, students' choices are narrowly confined. These three factors conspire to guarantee uninspired researchers, not passionate active searchers.

The Importance of Immersion

To ensure active research, students' questions should grow out of a compelling period of immersion. In an I-Search Unit, the period of immersion lasts two or three weeks. In this phase, teachers engage students in a set of coherent activities related to the theme's content. The content is derived from the theme and overarching concepts of the I-Search Unit. The activities are motivating—engaging all the senses, drawing on students' varied intelligences and talents.

Each activity has two goals. Teachers want students to develop a knowledge base related to the theme and concepts. At the same time, however, they also want to provoke and tantalize students, instilling in them a hunger to learn more. Ariel's questions in the previous quote did not

materialize out of thin air. Her teachers labored at crafting a coherent set of activities around the unit's theme of technology. As Ariel and her classmates learned more, they became further intrigued and motivated to gather additional information. Macrorie (1988) believes that it is not the student choosing the topic, but rather an issue, concern, or question that chooses the student. This was the case with Ariel and her classmates in Lawrence, New York. Figure 2.1 (see p. 20) lists some of their questions and traces them back to the specific content that hooked them during an immersion activity.

Developing a question from a strong knowledge base benefits young adolescents in two ways. First, it increases their chances to become self-directed learners who feel a sense of power and mastery over what they are learning. A language arts teacher noted that when inquiry grew out of immersion,

> The kids are picking questions that they are passionate about—this passion stuff is making a difference. They are engaged in the question; they have some control over it. They are benefiting from being able to make some decisions for themselves.

Second, when students generate a question they care about, based on immersion, the world of school becomes more authentic. School begins to model what happens in the real world of work, community, and home. As one student noted, "It's just what my father [a scientist] does. He finds a problem to be working on." Over time, another student recognized the significance of her work in today's world: "Why are we learning this? So we understand. And maybe something can be done."

FIGURE 2.1
I-Search Questions Based on Immersion Activities in I-Search Unit on Technology

Topic	Content in Immersion Activity	I-Search Question
Submarine Exploration	• Submarines helped find remains of many sunken ships • Submarines expanded our knowledge of the ocean	In what ways do submarines expand our knowledge of the geography of the ocean?
Diabetes	• Diabetes occurs when the body doesn't produce enough insulin for the body to absorb sugar	How has technology aided people diagnosed with diabetes?
Construction of Airplanes	• There are different kinds of airplanes • Different materials are used to build airplanes	How does the construction of airplanes change as technology changes?
Forensic Science	• Explanation of DNA • Definition of forensic science • Steps taken to find a missing person	In what ways can age enhancers help to capture missing people?

Immersion in Practice

To show immersion in practice, we draw on the work of a 6th grade interdisciplinary team from Bedford, Massachusetts. The teachers on this team taught language arts, social studies, science, and mathematics. A special education resource room teacher was also a team member who co-taught with the language arts teacher. I worked closely with the entire team as they participated in the research project on the effect of I-Search on middle school students.

The unit's theme was "How the Atlantic Ocean Affects the New England Economy: Past, Present, and Future." The subtext of the theme was that many different businesses and industries in New England are involved in developing, producing, and distributing goods and services related to the Atlantic Ocean. Their success or failure affects the economy. Figure 2.2 presents the unit's theme and overarching concepts.

This is a strong interdisciplinary theme because it draws on key concepts and skills identified in the *Curriculum Standards for Social Studies* (National Council for the Social Studies, 1994) and *National Science Education Standards* (National Research Council, 1996). The theme focused on the following concepts:

• Concepts about the roles played by supply and demand, prices, incentives, and profits in determining what is produced and distributed in a competitive market system.

• Economic concepts that help to explain historic and current developments and issues in local, national, or global contexts (e.g., studying the shipping industry over time).

• Concepts about the interrelationships among populations, resources, and environments, as well as natural hazards (e.g., pollutants in water).

• Geographic concepts and map skills.

The following is a day-by-day description of the three-week immersion activities in Bedford:

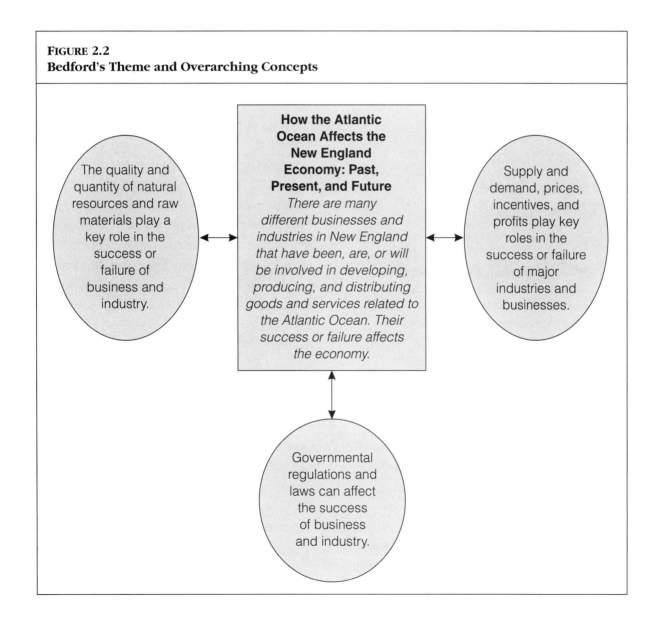

FIGURE 2.2
Bedford's Theme and Overarching Concepts

How the Atlantic Ocean Affects the New England Economy: Past, Present, and Future
There are many different businesses and industries in New England that have been, are, or will be involved in developing, producing, and distributing goods and services related to the Atlantic Ocean. Their success or failure affects the economy.

The quality and quantity of natural resources and raw materials play a key role in the success or failure of business and industry.

Supply and demand, prices, incentives, and profits play key roles in the success or failure of major industries and businesses.

Governmental regulations and laws can affect the success of business and industry.

Week 1

Monday: Chocolate manufacturing
activity

Tuesday: Chocolate manufacturing
activity (continued)

Wednesday: New England map activity

Thursday: Georges Bank activity

Friday: *Captains Courageous* (movie)

Week 2

Monday: Article: "Swimming May Be
Hazardous to Your Health"

Tuesday: Boston Harbor Activity

Wednesday: Speaker: Meg Tabasco
(Massachusetts Water Resources
Authority)

Thursday: Article: "Hook, Line, and
Sunk"

Friday: National Geographic video

Week 3

Monday: New England Aquarium field
trip

Tuesday: Coastal New England Getaway
activity

Wednesday: Speaker: Naturalist Richard
Wheeler; and Public Broadcasting
Service NOVA video

Thursday: Speaker from the Massachusetts Maritime Academy

Friday: Begin posing questions

Immersion began with two large context-
setting activities. Teachers designed the choco-
late-manufacturing activity to introduce students
to economic concepts (e.g., supply and demand,
production, sales and marketing, and profit).
Their second activity was aimed at providing students with basic geographic information about
the New England states that bordered the Atlantic
Ocean. All the teachers simultaneously carried
out these and other activities. Phase I ended with
a series of activities aimed at helping each

student pose an I-Search question.

The immersion activities embodied the following four characteristics: The activities were
directly related to the theme and overarching
concepts of the unit; used a variety of materials
and resources to engage students; were meaningfully sequenced to build conceptual understanding over time; and were held together with
strong instructional glue.

Immersion Activities Directly Related to the Theme and Overarching Concepts

It is not by chance that each immersion activity related to one or more of the overarching
concepts (see Figure 2.3) and led students back
to consider economic issues. When we designed
the immersion activities during curriculum design
(see Chapter 6), we evaluated each potential
activity against a set of criteria. One criterion was:
Does the activity help students understand the
overarching concepts? Many activities, although
interesting, were discarded when our answer to
this question was an unequivocal "No." Given
that immersion lasts for only two or three weeks,
we agreed that each activity must be conceptually weighted, which one teacher, Lynda, defined
as being "so juicy that it drips with content."

The activity that introduced students to
Georges Bank is a good example of a content-
rich activity that related to all three overarching
concepts. Two science teachers on the team,
Bradd and Carl, summarized the important content related to Georges Bank, as follows:

Georges Bank, located off the coast
of Massachusetts, is one of the richest
fisheries found anywhere in the world.

FIGURE 2.3
Immersion Activities Directly Connect to the Overarching Concepts

Activity	Natural resources play a key role in how the Atlantic Ocean affects the New England Economy.	Governmental regulations have an effect on how the Atlantic Ocean affects the New England economy.	Supply and demand have an effect on how the Atlantic Ocean affects the New England economy.
Chocolate Manufacturing Activity			✔
New England Map Activity	✔		
Georges Bank Activity	✔	✔	✔
Captains Courageous (movie)	✔		✔
Article: "Swimming May Be Hazardous to Your Health"	✔		
Boston Harbor Activity	✔	✔	
Speaker, Meg Tabasco (MWRA)	✔	✔	
Article: "Hook, Line, and Sunk"	✔	✔	✔
Video by National Geographic on Gloucester Fisherman	✔	✔	✔
Visit to New England Aquarium	✔	✔	
Coastal Getaway Activity	✔		✔
Speaker, Naturalist Richard Wheeler	✔	✔	
Speaker from Massachusetts Maritime Academy	✔	✔	

The bank is a form of sandbar, an underwater shelf where the water is shallow. The Labrador Current brings cold water down from the Arctic. When the cold, deep water currents hit the shallow banks, the nutrient-rich water from the ocean bottom is brought to the surface for the plankton to feed on. Plankton are microscopic organisms that drift in the ocean currents and serve as the basis for the food chain. Haddock, flounder, clams, mussels, and lobsters eat the plankton. This effect is magnified by the Gulf Stream, which brings warm water up north from the tropics. The plankton grow and multiply faster in the warmer temperatures. Dangerous crosscurrents occur in the area due to the mixing of the major currents. Giant eddies can occur unpredictably. Navigation hence can be rather treacherous, especially since the weather is often foggy. Because of overfishing in this area, the fish population is depleted. Recent legislation, which placed severe limitations on fishing in this area, was recently passed. Related implications are that the fishermen who have earned their livelihood by fishing in Georges Bank are now without work. As a result, consumers are facing higher prices for fish.

The other teachers on the team relied on this content as they carried out the activity.

Immersion Activities Use a Variety of Materials and Resources to Engage Students

Varied materials and resources allow students to engage in content in different ways and from different perspectives. For example, the Georges Bank activity easily lent itself to using maps, photographs, videos, newspaper articles, books, and an audiotape of an interview aired on National Public Radio (NPR).

Classroom walls are no barrier to immersion activities. Teachers invite speakers to school to share their expertise, relate personal anecdotes, and give real-world examples. Field trips outside of school allow students to have hands-on experiences. By using varied media inside and outside of school, teachers can more effectively build on students' diverse strengths, learning styles, and multiple intelligences. For example, teachers can show documentaries to graphically present specific information and have students perform an experiment or engage in a simulation. By embedding music, art, drama, and experiments into instruction, teachers can reach students whose strengths may lie in linguistic, logical-mathematical, spatial, bodily-kinesthetic, musical, interpersonal, or intrapersonal intelligences (Gardner, 1983, 1993).

The Bedford teachers relied on self-imposed guidelines to ensure use of varied materials and resources in planning their immersion activities. They determined what they wanted students to read (e.g., books, magazines, newspaper articles, materials downloaded from the Internet), watch (e.g., videos), to whom they could ask questions (e.g., in a structured interview or survey), and what students could do (e.g., experiment, go on a field trip, do a simulation). *Read, watch, ask,* and *do* are the same categories that the teachers would later introduce to students for the design of research plans (see Chapter 3). Figure 2.4 shows how the Bedford immersion activities fall within these four categories of materials and resources.

FIGURE 2.4
Use of Varied Materials and Resources in Immersion Activities

Activity	Reading Varied Materials	Watching or Viewing	Asking People Questions (Interviews & Surveys)	Doing an Experiment or Taking a Field Trip
Chocolate Manufacturing Activity	✔			✔
New England Map Activity	✔		✔	
Georges Bank Activity	✔	✔		✔
Movie: *Captains Courageous*		✔		
Article: "Swimming May Be Hazardous to Your Health"	✔			
Boston Harbor Activity	✔			
Speaker, Meg Tabasco		✔	✔	✔
Article: "Hook, Line, and Sunk"	✔			
Video by National Geographic on Gloucester Fisherman		✔		
Visit to New England Aquarium	✔	✔	✔	✔
Coastal Getaway Activity	✔	✔	✔	
Speaker, Naturalist Richard Wheeler		✔	✔	
Speaker, Massachusetts Maritime Academy		✔	✔	

Most of these immersion activities were multidimensional, relying on varied materials and resources. The two-day "Coastal New England Getaway" activity provides a good example. The goal of the activity was for students to build knowledge about tourism, a cornerstone of New England's economy. Teachers asked students to form small, cooperative groups, with each group representing a simulated family. Teachers explained:

> You are going on an imaginary weekend getaway with your "school family." This trip begins Friday following eighth period, and you will return to Bedford on Sunday evening. It is important that you research your trip before leaving and plan your activities carefully because you will have a limited amount of money. Have fun!

Students needed to work with a fixed budget and allocate money for designated costs—transportation, accommodations, dining, sightseeing, recreation, and incidentals. To help each family group plan and budget for their trip, teachers distributed maps and tourist guides of New England (e.g., *AAA Guide*, *Fodors*, and *Mobil Guide*). Some groups supplemented their reading of these books with watching videos and calling Chambers of Commerce, hotels, and tourist attractions. They also polled family and friends for their opinions of the best of New England. At the end of two days, each group described where they went, what they had done, and what they had spent on this pretend trip. They used maps, spreadsheets, photographs, and writings as part of their group presentations.

Another good example of a multidimensional activity was a presentation by Meg Tabasco, an invited speaker from the Massachusetts Water Resources Authority (MWRA). She spoke about the past pollution and current cleanup efforts of the Boston Harbor. She talked about the cycle of water (from toilet to pipes to sewer systems), the amount of waste that travels through the system, the natural process of waste disposal, and the purpose of a treatment plant and how it works. Relying heavily on student questions and input to structure her presentation, she invited students to manipulate materials (e.g., poster boards with Velcro images). She even distributed fertilizer pellets made from recycled waste materials (which turned out to be a big hit). At the end, she gave each student a beautifully prepared folder with six booklets. Students appreciated her effective presentation style:

> Meg Tabasco . . . made things fun and interesting. She did that by letting kids go up to the board and draw stuff and she was funny. The kids also got to ask and answer questions.

Immersion Activities Are Meaningfully Sequenced to Build Conceptual Understanding Over Time

Conceptual understanding expands over time, emerging from prior knowledge and solidifying through exposure and feedback (Zahorik, 1997). Across the three weeks of immersion, the Bedford team wanted students to build and expand their conceptual understanding from one activity to another. Thus, the sequence of the activities was extremely important, because some concepts laid the foundation for others. For example, teachers planned a cluster of activities near the beginning of Phase I that involved learning about Georges Bank, viewing the movie

Captains Courageous, reading articles about pollution in Boston, Harbor, learning about the history of Boston Harbor, and hearing Meg Tabasco. Figure 2.5 shows how concepts built from one activity to another. For example, the Georges Bank activity contributed to an understanding of why the bank was a rich fishing area; and the film *Captains Courageous* enriched this understanding and helped students understand the economic factors that contribute to fishing.

To create a widening spiral of concept building, teachers expanded on concepts introduced earlier in this phase of immersion. For example, just before the unit began, teachers gave each student a blank map of New England with the coastline highlighted in bold. With help from their families, students wrote in all of the coastal towns and cities they had ever visited. They also jotted down what they had done there and how much the activity had cost. This exercise later served as the foundation for the Coastal New England Getaway activity, where students delved more deeply into the cost of recreation. In short, students expanded their knowledge of places to

---

FIGURE 2.5
Concept Building Across Immersion Activities

Activity	Concepts
Georges Bank	• understanding the geography and ecology of Georges Bank • understanding why Georges Bank was a rich fishing area • understanding factors related to the depletion of fish in Georges Bank • understanding governmental laws concerning overfishing and the protection of fishing areas
Captains Courageous (movie)	• understanding economic factors that contribute to fishing • understanding uses of the Boston Harbor Islands and Boston Harbor and how this affects the economy
Past Use of Boston Harbor Islands for Recreation	• understanding factors that caused pollution in the Boston Harbor and the Islands • understanding the impact of pollution on the economy
Pollution in Boston Harbor	• understand the efforts to clean up the Boston Harbor and the financial costs
Meg Tabasco—Boston Harbor Cleanup	• understanding the economic impact of the Boston Harbor cleanup on New England

visit, tourism, and economic implications by building on knowledge acquired from a previous activity.

Immersion Activities Are Held Together with Strong Instructional Glue

Teachers used the following three instructional strategies to glue the activities together: elicit prior knowledge; help students extract and relate relevant information; and encourage and guide students to process information by reflecting on what they are learning and thinking. Cooperative learning was an integral part of the instructional process.

Elicit Prior Knowledge. What students learn depends on their previous understanding, the ways they perceive and organize the world, and the current context (Smith, 1995). Learners generate meaning as they construct relationships among their knowledge; their memories of experience; and what they are doing, reading, hearing, or observing (Wittrock, 1986). In Phase I, teachers build into each activity a time to elicit students' prior knowledge. The Bedford teachers jokingly called this the "Velcro Theory." When they elicited prior knowledge, they imagined a Velcro band forming around a student's head. The new information was the second piece of Velcro, which then easily adhered to the first. They even used this metaphor with students to make the teaching/learning process explicit.

At the outset of the unit, teachers wanted to find out, in broad strokes, how student knowledge mapped onto the theme and overarching concepts. They asked, "What are students' starting points? What do they already know? What

prior information will facilitate concept building?" By listening carefully, teachers heard the following from their students:

> In 5th grade we learned a lot about the whales. I didn't really do much about the Atlantic Ocean. But I've gone to a lot of beaches. We also learned about Thompson's Island. I went to Thompson's Island once.
>
> Foreign people who come to Boston spend money. That gives more money to Boston.
>
> I know that many jobs come from it [Atlantic Ocean] and that lots of people pollute it. We are trying to help that problem. Things that are on the coast sometimes help their business.
>
> There are people who want to stop the fisherman from fishing in the Boston Harbor. If they do that, it would affect the fisherman, the boatmakers, and well maybe the seafood restaurants because they would need fish.

In addition to hearing students' overall starting points, teachers also elicited students' specific prior knowledge at the beginning of each activity. For example, before the Boston Harbor activity, students talked about which islands in the harbor they had visited, when, and why. This preparation allowed students to make more meaning out of their experiences.

Extract and Relate Relevant Information. Teachers introduced specific strategies aimed at helping students process new information, regardless if the activity involved reading, going on a field trip, listening to speakers, or watching videos. For example, after reading the magazine article, "Hook, Line, and Sunk," students listed key events identified in the article on separate index cards and then sequenced the cards in chronological order. This helped them understand the rise and fall of the fishing industry over time, as well as cause and effect relationships. In the Georges Bank activity, students drew maps to help them understand what happens when warm and cold currents meet. When students watched *Captains Courageous*, teachers used a strategy called a "data dump." At predetermined intervals, the teachers paused the movie. For three minutes, students were asked to write everything they remembered about the previous segment of the movie. "Don't worry about spelling or punctuation—just get the ideas down," the teachers explained. After the movie, students worked in small groups, referring to their notes to relate ideas in the movie to the thematic web. Later, students reworked the rough text into formalized notes that made sense.

Teachers helped students relate information from one activity to another through discussion, writing, drawing, and making webs. At one point, one student explained:

> We learned about industry and business—how it works and the things they have to do. So in the fishing industry, they would have to pay for ice fishing materials and boats. There are a lot of jobs that have to do with that. Most of the industries are going out of business because of the decrease in the fish.

Teachers also continued to expand the original web that presented the unit's theme and overarching concepts. Over time, each overarching concept became more fully elaborated as students added specific content based on what they learned (see Figure 2.6, on p. 30). The goal was to connect the growing information map to each student's own mental map, interconnecting ideas to perceive relationships.

Process and Reflect. In an interview presented in *Educational Leadership* (Pool, 1997), Renate Nummela Caine asserted that "children learn best if they are immersed in complex experiences and are given the opportunity to actively process what they have learned" (p. 14). The Bedford teachers, not wanting their students to move nonstop from activity to activity, recognized that students needed time set aside between activities for processing and reflection. Although not recorded in the daily schedule presented earlier, processing and reflection took place almost daily so that students would grasp the implications of what they were learning. Processing through reflection is powerful because it creates a learning loop, an important element for higher-order thinking (Caine & Caine, 1991).

The teachers explicitly stated the need for personal reflection. Sal, the social studies teacher, explained to his students that meaning making was individualistic. He carefully chose his words as he said, "What one student is thinking is different from everyone else, because past knowledge and experiences affect the way new information is perceived."

By posing a set of prompting questions, teachers helped students to process information. At the beginning of an activity, teachers asked students what they already knew and what more they wanted to find out. Afterward, teachers asked students to reflect on what they had found interesting and what more they wanted to know based on what they had just learned. Many teachers used the following open-ended questions for reflection:

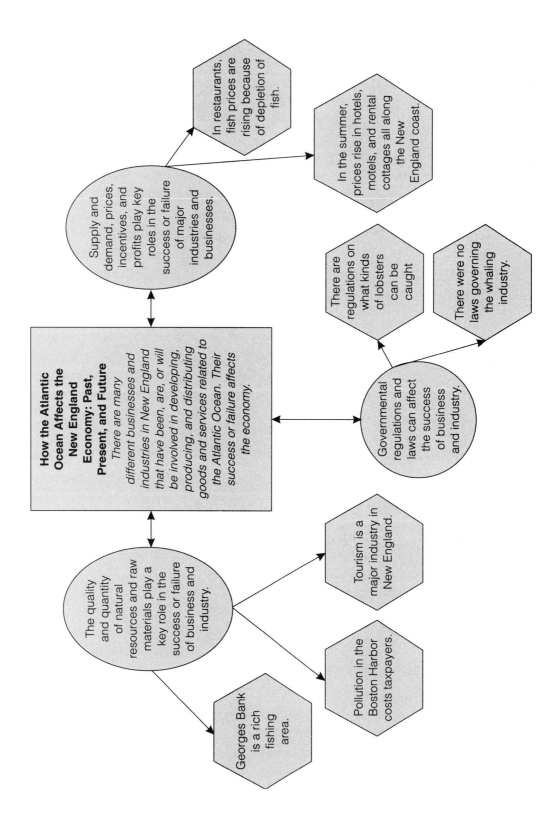

FIGURE 2.6
Bedford's Theme and Overarching Concepts Elaborated with Content

How the Atlantic Ocean Affects the New England Economy: Past, Present, and Future
There are many different businesses and industries in New England that have been, are, or will be involved in developing, producing, and distributing goods and services related to the Atlantic Ocean. Their success or failure affects the economy.

Supply and demand, prices, incentives, and profits play key roles in the success or failure of major industries and businesses.

In restaurants, fish prices are rising because of depletion of fish.

In the summer, prices rise in hotels, motels, and rental cottages all along the New England coast.

Governmental regulations and laws can affect the success of business and industry.

There are regulations on what kinds of lobsters can be caught

There were no laws governing the whaling industry.

The quality and quantity of natural resources and raw materials play a key role in the success or failure of business and industry.

Georges Bank is a rich fishing area.

Tourism is a major industry in New England.

Pollution in the Boston Harbor costs taxpayers.

Something interesting I learned is . . .
I learned this from . . .
The part of the web this relates to is . . .
This made me think about . . .
I would like to learn more about . . .

After an immersion activity, teachers in Bedford asked students to respond to these questions on the computer using the *Search Organizer* software. Figure 2.7 (see p. 32) provides an example of how one student used the computer-based template to reflect on Meg Tabasco's presentation on sewage and the water cycle.

Another good strategy for capturing reflections is asking students to keep a handwritten or online journal. Almost like a diary, this becomes a private place for students to record their innermost thoughts. Young adolescents rather enjoy keeping a diary or journal and do not usually consider it to be a burden. One of the world's most famous young diarists, Anne Frank, is a poignant example. The Anne Frank Museum in Amsterdam displays her actual diary, and next to it are her words, "Unless you write yourself, you can't know how wonderful it is."

Building on middle schoolers' natural inclination to document their thinking, teachers introduce diarylike journals to young adolescents at the outset of Phase I. Teachers explain that the journal will be a place for students to chronicle events, reflect on what they are learning, and explore their personal responses to content. The journal can serve as a sourcebook of ideas, thoughts, observations, opinions, and questions that can be mined for later use in processing information (Parsons, 1990). One student in New Hampshire found the journal invaluable:

> The most important thing I learned was to always keep a journal during the search. I had it as a resource to use; everything was in my journal—beginning to end. I could use it when I needed to go back.

Bedford teachers were generous about giving students time to write in their journals before and after immersion activities. For example, one student made the following journal entry after Meg Tabasco's visit:

> If they don't clean the fish well enough, the fish will probably be affected by the bacteria or the toxic waste. She [Meg Tabasco] talked about polluting the water and how it's going to kill the fish and it's going to poison us. It's sort of like "what goes around comes around." The fishing industry would be affected if the fish were polluted. They would probably be sued by families because they would get illnesses.

As in this entry, students can bring to the surface thoughts that help them to make connections. Frequent journal writing allows for the expansion of personal ideas, impressions, perspectives, and feelings. From their ongoing reflections, students generate questions that stem from their personal interests.

Question-Posing in Practice

> Get a strong question that you know a lot about already—not too much about it but that you've heard something about it. You want to make sure it's a really strong question and it has a lot of different parts. Make sure it relates to the web.

FIGURE 2.7
Screens Showing How *Search Organizer* Helps Students to Reflect on Speaker

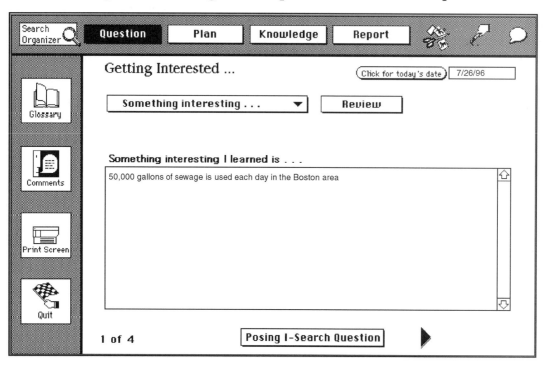

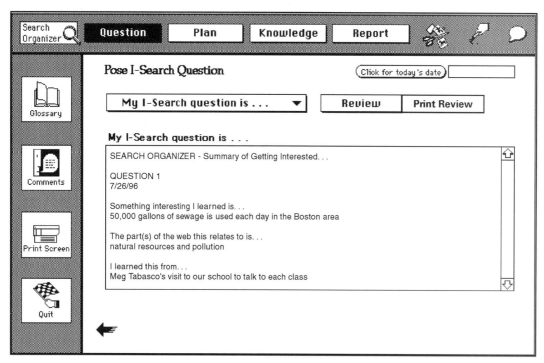

> You really need to care about your
> question. It will be your life for the next
> six weeks.

As highlighted in the preceding comments by two Bedford students, a good I-Search question has the following characteristics:

- It relates to the theme and overarching concepts.
- It reveals the student's passionate interest.
- It is researchable by gathering information from varied resources and materials.

Teachers do not keep these criteria secret; they emblazon them in every student's mind by posting them on the bulletin board, handing them out to students, announcing them to parents, and giving students a chance to talk about them. Although these criteria let students know what they are aiming for, it is the teacher's role to ensure that students meet these criteria. To this end, the teachers in Bedford developed four instructional strategies to help students pose questions. Teachers provide ample opportunity to practice posing questions throughout Phase I; they provide models for posing questions; they give feedback on student's draft questions; and they provide tools to support the ongoing work.

Teachers Give Ample Opportunity to Practice

Bedford teachers understood that each activity had the potential to be provocative. Therefore, they made question-posing a habit before, during, and after each activity. Before an activity, questions were predictive in nature; teachers guided students to ask "What if?" types of questions. During the activity, questions helped

students stay focused, extract relevant information, and relate new information to past experiences. After an activity, teachers asked students to summarize, asking, "What did you learn?" and then adding, "What more do you want to know?"

Teachers Provide Models for Posing Questions

Teachers need to buttress criteria with good examples to convey what is really valued. One way to provide students with models is for teachers to "think aloud" as they, themselves, pose a question. By listening as their teachers make their own cognitive processing explicit, students can observe an adult's "in flight" thinking, drafting, and editing of a question (Morocco & Zorfass, 1996).

Marilyn, the mathematics teacher, used this approach. She explained to her class that one student, Derek, had been talking about the closing down of Hanscom Air Force Base, located in Bedford. This, she said, made her think about the ripple effect the closing would have on the town and state's economy. She compared this event to recent class discussions about the depressed economy in the old whaling town of New Bedford where many fisherman had lost their livelihoods. There, the ripple effect was that stores and restaurants were shutting down due to a lack of customers and business. She told her students that as they were pursuing their I-Searches, she wanted to do her own search on this question: "How does the town government help merchants once a military base closes?"

Many teachers employ another strategy; they use the students' emerging questions as grist for the mill. Teachers in Bedford maintained running lists of questions on bulletin boards and chalkboards. Here are a few of these emerging questions:

- What is nature's own ability to clean up polluted waters?
- What will be the marine engineering jobs in the future?
- What is the same and different about catching fish in the past and present?
- How does human trash kill marine life?
- What is the future of Georges Bank?
- What are some of the modern advancements in fishing/technology?
- What is the foreign competition in fishing?
- What are the jobs related to treating polluted waters?

Because the class as a whole owned these questions, teachers could repeatedly refer to them and help the class revise them. Any student could later draw on one or more of the public questions when generating his or her own question.

Teachers Give Feedback on Draft Questions

Bedford teachers realized that students needed a chance to draft questions based on criteria and then receive feedback from teachers and classmates. Effective feedback finds the kernel of a good idea and helps to shape it. Diplomacy is necessary to ensure that students do not lose a sense of ownership over their inquiry processes. For example, one teacher, Marie,

explained how she tried to be sensitive to a student's needs while trying to ensure success:

> I know one student who wanted to do oil spills in New England. And yes, there have been oil spills in New England, but the stretch you have to make, in my opinion (knowing the student), from looking at oil spills and then to trying to see their impact on New England's economy, is too big. She needs something more concrete to start off with, because I think in this type of project everybody needs to be successful.

To ensure that this student's question would not lead her on a frustrating journey, Marie met with her to review her journal, discuss her interests, and review the class list of emerging questions. This kind of support gave ownership back to the student, who later generated a question about tourism that met all three criteria—to relate to the theme and overarching concepts, to reveal the student's passionate interest, and to be researchable.

Teachers have found that students have a talent for critiquing one another's emerging questions. Marcia, the language arts teacher, organized her students into cooperative groups for this purpose. She urged them to be "critical friends." "It's OK to argue about how a question is related to the web," she explained.

In another classroom, teachers and small groups of students discussed questions that were too broad or too narrow. For example, here is a question that other students deemed too broad: "In the past 100 years, what are all of the industries in New England that use or have used the Atlantic Ocean, and what resources have they used?" Another student recommended a solution: "Why not focus on a specific time period?"

Other questions needed help because they were too narrow (e.g., "When will the Boston Harbor cleanup be finished?"). To "plump up" this question, one student suggested exploring the economic, environmental, and political factors affecting the completion of the cleanup.

Teachers asked students to submit one or more draft questions. The team of teachers worked together to evaluate students' draft questions and provide feedback. Here are several of the student's draft questions:

> How does the lobster industry affect the economy of New England's coastline? How has the ship building in Maine affected New England's jobs, present, past, and future?
> How have the environmental laws preserved the lobster in the past, present, and future?
> How do oil spills affect harbor seals?

Lynda, the language arts teacher, brought questions like this to a team meeting. She and her colleagues read aloud each student's question. The teachers worked together to assign each question to one of three piles: "OK," "needs a little help," and "needs a lot of help." For example, the preceding question about how oil spills affect harbor seals was placed in the "needs a lot of help" category because it had no relationship to the economy. Questions placed in that category received written feedback in the form of suggestions and probing questions. For example, Carl explains how he gave support and guidance to a student's draft question on clamming:

> Here is a student who listed clamming as a topic. She didn't really have a

question, only a topic. So I suggested that she consider: What caused the clamming beds to close down? What has been done to clean them up? What is the future for clam farms? How might this effect the economy?

Because the team promised feedback to their 125 students within 24 hours, the teachers were forced to work quickly and efficiently. They found that by working as a team to collaboratively review questions, they were able to make a labor-intensive process meaningful for them and worthwhile for their students.

Teachers Use Tools to Support the Process

Teachers gave students tools to support the question-posing process. Marilyn distributed a guide sheet that prompted students to review their notes, reflect on their interests, and discuss their ideas and concerns with the teacher and their classmates (see Figure 2.8, on p. 36):

Other teachers also used the prompting questions available on the *Search Organizer:*

- My question is . . .
- I care about this question because . . .
- My starting point is . . .

These questions provided a safety net for students to begin to document their thinking. Here is an example of one student's thinking:

> My I-Search question is, How does Georges Bank affect the New England economy and the fishing industry? I care about this question because a lot of people get their jobs from Georges Bank. If it didn't exist, there would not be a fishing industry in New England. I think that Georges Bank is very important and we

---

FIGURE 2.8
Guide for Students as They Pose Research Questions

---

1. After reviewing my notes, thinking about what I saw and read, and then discussing facts/ideas with my group, I have decided I want to know more about _____
_____
_____

2. I thought about this topic because _____
_____
_____

3. After thinking about my topic some more, I checked in with my group and the teacher to create an exciting, passionate, interesting, and informative question that I will investigate further and report back to the class by the end of three weeks. Comments: _____
_____
_____

4. My question is _____
_____
_____

---

need to stop overfishing if we want to continue fishing there. As a starting point, I already know how Georges Bank was formed. It is a big sand bank that has an enormous effect on the New England coast. Georges Bank is in worse condition than the Canadian fishing grounds, and overfishing isn't helping it.

Teachers Make Questions Public

Once everyone in the class had a firm question, Bradd, like the other teachers, posted the questions on the bulletin board that displayed the web of the theme and overarching concepts. He hung each question next to its relevant overarching concept.

By making student work public, teachers conveyed that every student's search question counted. As one teacher explained, "We need information from each student's search to answer our overarching questions." The public display of questions offered another benefit: Both students and teachers could see where questions overlapped. Then, teachers could create cooperative groups, or students could seek each other out to share resources, exchange information, and help each other process information.

Final Comments

Phase I is a time set aside for teachers to help students build knowledge based on what they already know, guide and support students so that a research question "finds them," and shape that question so that students can begin their own personal investigation. Over the course of a few weeks, students' ideas and questions evolve. For example, one student in Bedford explains:

> We started off with the guest speaker Meg Tabasco. In the beginning, I thought I might do a search on the MWRA . . . but then we saw a National Geographic video that said some things about the 200-mile limit. That really stuck to me. I promised myself that I would somehow relate to the 200-mile limit. I finally narrowed it down to 'How have the environmental laws passed in the 1970s helped and improved New England waters, and how does this affect the economy?"

Even though students end the immersion phase with a research question, and these questions are posted for all to see, teachers remind students: "Your question is not etched in stone. Through the inquiry process, a clearer or more interesting question might emerge. It's OK to change your question. This is what it means to be an active researcher."

One criterion for posing a good question is that the question forces students to use varied materials and resources. The next chapter focuses on how this can be achieved—and how students can travel beyond the safety of trusted encyclopedias.

Accessing Varied
Materials and Resources

During the search process, I discovered that encyclopedias and books are good for background information—but to get good, current, accurate prices and other economic information, you must do "real" research. The best ways to get information are to write some letters, talk to people on the phone, and visit some places or sites.

Goals for Young Adolescents

The previous quote comes from Kevin, a student in Bedford, who was investigating lobstering. He visited Al King, the owner of a lobster company in Gloucester; called Bill Alder, executive director of the Massachusetts Lobsterman's Association; wrote nine letters to lobster companies and hatcheries; and conducted telephone interviews with various people involved with the industry. This student epitomizes the proactive researcher: He expends time and exerts energy to seek out varied materials and resources. We could imagine Kevin, residing on the East Coast, nodding in agreement with the sentiments expressed by an active researcher from the Midwest and another from the West Coast:

Things aren't going to come to you; you have to go to them. I had to search through lots of things before I got what I really needed.

I learned that information isn't always handed to you. Sometimes you really have to dig to find a good piece of information.

One I-Search goal is for students to dig deeply by accessing information that falls within four categories:

- *Reading* a variety of printed matter (e.g., fiction and nonfiction books, periodicals, reference materials, and brochures) and accessing information from Web sites on the Internet.
- *Asking* people for information (e.g., conducting interviews, conducting surveys, and posting and receiving messages on the Internet).
- *Watching* or viewing (e.g., videos, television shows, slides, and CD-ROMs).
- *Doing* an activity or participating in an event (e.g., conducting an experiment, visiting a museum, working with a computer simulation, accessing a database, and taking photographs).

Knowing that students need as many powerful routes to learning as possible, teachers open new doors to exploration when they explicitly tell students that they must *read, watch, ask,* and *do.* For young adolescents who are used to relying on a single source of information (most likely the encyclopedia), this is an eye-opening concept, as one Bedford student stated:

> Before (when we were doing a project in the earlier grades) . . . it was just "go look in the encyclopedia and copy down information." But now, I've learned how to get information in different ways and get more up-to-date stuff by calling people, visiting people, and . . . writing letters. And it's much more effective than just looking in the encyclopedia that's 20 years old.

Using the *read, ask, watch,* and *do* guidelines, students begin to recognize their own hidden talents and potential. This is what happened to one student in Bedford who discovered that interviewing was a potent way to access information.

> Many new skills have improved. . . . As I said before, not all the information I needed was in the books I used, so I had to call and ask anyone anything that they knew about pollution on Cape Cod. . . . I had to reach out to everyone; even people I did not know. (I feel a lot better now that I have expanded my horizon.)

Accessing information from various sources affords students the chance to gather multiple perspectives. This is valuable for the young adolescent who is just beginning to relinquish a single world view. For example, two students in Bedford were investigating the deep sea fishing industry in Massachusetts. Each had gone to a different scuba diving shop to interview the owners and managers. When the students met to pool what they had learned, they discovered conflicting information. This experience taught them an important lesson, "You probably need to ask several people the same question and not just rely on one response."

Whereas our overall goal is for young adolescents to learn how to access information by reading, watching, asking, and doing, we can identify five subgoals that can lead to achieving the broader goal, as follows:

1. *Using Information-Gathering Skills.* Before the I-Search Unit begins, students need to acquire, practice, and apply information-gathering skills. These skills include locating information in a library, knowing how to conduct an interview, knowing how to construct survey questions, using microfiche, and using search engines on the Internet to locate Web sites of value.

2. *Forming a Search Plan.* Once students pose their I-Search question at the end of Phase

I, teachers want them to be able to design a search plan. The plan, developed in Phase II, explicitly lists what they intend to read, watch, ask, and do, and the order in which they plan to do this.

3. *Modifying the Search*. As students carry out their plans in Phase III, they need to be able to make modifications as they discover new sources of information, change direction after reaching a dead end, or revise their question based on new insights. For example, one group of students working together as a cooperative group learned unexpectedly that an elementary teacher in their town had just completed an extensive unit on wetlands, their very topic. When they visited her after school, she lent them a set of useful books and directed them to the wetland directly behind her school. They immediately proceeded to the wetland to observe wildlife, take photographs, make a list of the trash left scattered about (e.g., plastic wrappers, oil barrels), and take pH readings at different spots (which they later displayed in a graph). Although none of these data sources was in their original plan, the information they obtained through exploration became the centerpiece of their investigation.

4. *Reflecting on the Search and Making Connections*. The fourth goal is for students to continue to reflect in their journals. The chronicling of their search helps them recognize connections among what they did, what they found, what content they learned, and what they learned about themselves as researchers. For example, a student in Lawrence, New York, who was investigating terrorism, made the following journal entry:

> When I tried to get an interview with the Federal Bureau of Investigation, I ran into some trouble. . . . But eventually I got through to this man named George Andrews. . . . I know now that I have to be tough when I get an interview, to not act desperate but to be kind and strong . . . . I also thought that taking down good interview questions will help me out when I grow up. Maybe I'll be a journalist, and I will have to interview somebody.

As students chronicle the story of their search, they can reflect on their progress at that time or later when they write their reports or prepare their exhibitions. In the section of the I-Search Unit called, "What This Means to Me," students are asked to consciously reflect on what they learned about accessing varied resources and materials. In the previous example, the student who focused on terrorism recognized this:

> From the interview that I took, I learned that I have to be a lot kinder to people if I want to get information in whatever I am studying. I also realized that the people that I am asking to have interviews with have lives too, and that they are not always there to help people like me get information. So I learned how to be patient, as well. . . . I took risks when I did my interview because I did not want to ask a question that was top secret and then they would hang up on me. I had to ask smart questions that would get good answers and that did not give away vital FBI information.

5. *Citing References*. Students need to learn how to cite references for two good reasons. First, if students themselves want to revisit and

check information or investigate their topic more deeply at a later time, they will know where to search. Second, clear references can facilitate the search by someone else who has become excited by the student's search and desires to know more. It is self-affirming for young adolescents to feel that they have motivated the active research of others. As Macrorie (1988) says:

> The purpose of bibliographies is to assist a reader who may get so interested in the topic that he or she wants to check further. They tell him where to go so he won't have to do all the hunting the I-Searcher did in order to find a good article (p. 65).

Accessing Materials and Resources in Practice

To ensure that students meet these goals, teachers take specific steps during curriculum design, before implementing the unit, and during all phases. Figure 3.1 (on p. 42) summarizes these practices and serves as the framework for the remainder of this chapter.

During Curriculum Design

During the early stages of the curriculum-design process, when teachers are on the verge of agreeing on a viable theme for their unit, they consider two questions:

• Will we be able to find a good selection of varied materials and resources for our Phase I immersion activities so that we can not only intrigue students and build their knowledge, but also model *read, watch, ask,* and *do?*

• Are we confident that abundant materials

and resources are available for students to access as they pursue their own questions?

By engaging in a minisearch, teachers can test out their assumptions about what resources and materials actually exist. The Bedford teachers had experienced difficulties in finding resources during the first year they used I-Search Units:

> *Marcia (language arts teacher):* Remember last spring? We didn't know what was there, and we sent them on this wild goose chase . . . . We've got to know what's there. We can't set ourselves or the kids up for failure.
> *Joan (librarian):* For a research process that demands such unusual research, to make repeated trips to this library where the information is *not,* is looking for trouble.

To overcome these difficulties, the Bedford team carried out the following activities to locate materials and resources related to how the New England economy is affected by the Atlantic Ocean:

• As a group, they met with Joan, the school librarian, to identify what was in the school library. Some teachers even asked Joan to help them brush up on their own skills in accessing information.

• They asked Joan to continue locating resources beyond their library. Joan then contacted the librarians at the high school, elementary schools, and the town library.

• As a group, the team went to the town library. The town librarian helped them make lists of information.

• They sought out small-town newspapers from coastal towns in New England because

FIGURE 3.1
Ways to Help Students Access Materials and Resources: Before and During the Unit

During Curriculum Design	Before Implementation	During Phase I	During Phase II	During Phase III	During Phase IV
• Teachers engage in a minisearch to test out assumptions about what is available and gather resources and materials • Teachers set criteria for student searches under the headings of *Read, Watch, Ask,* and *Do*	• Teachers and librarians/media specialists preteach library skills • Teachers help students to practice new skills in mini-units	• Teachers model *Read, Watch, Ask* and *Do* and make this explicit to students	• Teachers guide students in developing a search plan	• Teachers make arrangements so that students have access to information • Teachers assess student performance and, as needed, provide support	• Teachers establish rubrics that guide students to describe their search process and reflect on what they have learned about being a researcher

these newspapers tended to feature articles about the plight of fishermen who inhabited their towns.

• They went on their own field trips, for example, to the Boston Aquarium, the New Bedford Whaling Museum, and a fish-processing plant.

• They listed and then contacted potential speakers and people students could interview.

• One teacher called National Public Radio (NPR) to request a tape of a featured segment on the decline of fishing in New England and impending federal legislation.

• The team found good literature to ensure that students would read more.

Teachers at the Crispus Attucks Middle School in Indianapolis, who also carried out their own out-of-school probing for a unit on the history of Indianapolis, found their minisearch invaluable:

The I-Search Unit has made me a better teacher because it's forced me, along with all of the other teachers in the group, to go out and learn a lot of new things myself. We've been making a lot of trips to libraries, and we've been going around town trying to figure out where we want to take field trips—visiting the Red Cross and talking about what they do. These kinds of things get you very excited as a teacher. A lot of people are talking about burnout and doing the same thing over and over again, but we don't have time to talk about those things. We're always doing something new.

After teachers complete their minisearch, they can more realistically set criteria for how many resources they will expect students to use. Telling students how many *reads, watches, asks,* and *do's* they are responsible for gives them clear guidelines—but leaves enough flexibility for young adolescents to take ownership of the active research process. In addition to the availability of resources, teachers also base their criteria on factors such as the student's grade and abilities, the theme and length of the unit, what information is available, and whether a student carries out his or her search only inside or also outside of school. Teachers model these activities during immersion (Phase I).

A typical expectation for 7th grade students is to read at least four types of textual materials; conduct at least one interview or a survey (in person, via the telephone, or on the Internet); view at least two different media; and do at least one activity. By using the term *at least,* teachers invite students to do much more than the base level of expectation. Many students discover they cannot help themselves from going beyond the minimum. As one student noted:

> I learned that I needed to get more information than I had to. I shouldn't just get what I was told to because sometimes it's not enough. Something you thought might be a source of information might turn out not to actually be a source. I needed to keep going . . . looking for more stuff.

Before Implementing the Unit

Teachers and media specialists can prevent the frustration that can easily engulf a developing active researcher who doesn't feel comfortable in a library or media center. If students lack the kinds of skills defined by the National Council for the Social Studies (1994), as shown in Figure 3.2 (see p. 44), then teachers need to preteach these skills and encourage students to practice using them in meaningful contexts.

Teachers Enhance Students' Library Skills. Early in the school year, before they implement an I-Search Unit, teachers often work with librarians to make sure that students develop needed skills. For example, in Lawrence, a language arts teacher and the media specialist planned two days of skill instruction. The focus of Day 1 was on using the card catalogue, locating materials in the stacks, and using microfiche. Day 2 focused on technology supports (e.g., CD-ROM encyclopedias and online databases). Students could choose to sign up for any or all of the minilessons, depending on what they already knew. Going even further, teachers in Indianapolis arranged for approximately 40 students to go on a field trip to the library at the Indiana University-Purdue University of Indiana. Teachers planned what they would do in school before the trip to prepare students (e.g., review a map of the library, set a purpose, review different ways to locate information); how they would work with the university librarians during the visit to maximize student productivity; and how they would debrief with students after the trip. Students later talked about how secure they felt using microfiche and databases because of this advance planning.

FIGURE 3.2
Essential Skills for Social Studies: Acquiring Information

Find Information

• Use various parts of a book (index, table of contents, etc.)
• Use keywords, letters on volumes, index, and cross-references to find information
• Evaluate sources of information—print, visual, electronic
• Use appropriate source of information
• Use the community as a resource

The Library

• Use card catalog to locate books
• Use *Reader's Guide to Periodical Literature* and other indexes
• Use COMCATS (Computer Catalog Service)
• Use public library telephone information

Source: National Council for the Social Studies. (1994). *Curriculum standards for social studies* (Appendix A, p. 148). Washington, DC: Author.

Teachers Preteach Interviewing Skills.
One important skill for an I-Search Unit that needs preteaching is interviewing. Macrorie (1988), a strong proponent of interviewing, advises researchers: "Go to people. They're alive this year, up to date (p. 89)." Learning how to be an effective interviewer resonates with both the curricular goals of middle school teachers and the developmental needs of young adolescents. At this stage, as young adolescents separate from their families, they become excited about talking to experts outside the immediate realm of home and school. The chance to contact and communicate with an outside expert is an adultlike

behavior. When done successfully, the young adolescent's self-esteem is bolstered, as shown by this student comment:

> I used to be afraid to interview people, so I either wouldn't call, or wouldn't ask all my questions. All of the interviewing that I had to do for this I-Search made me less afraid. Now I can acquire more information.

Teachers emphasize that a good interview should yield relevant, current, and detailed information. To help students conduct interviews that reach this standard, teachers need to teach students *how* to interview before they schedule their first appointments. Some teachers have guided students through a three-step approach, as follows:

• Teachers help students set the context for an upcoming interview, asking them to list their goals, the name of the person they intend to interview, what they already know about this person, and what they want to learn from the interview.

• Teachers help students formulate pointed interview questions.

• Teachers show students the importance of certain procedures, or logistics.

For example, before the interview, students learn to confirm the date and time, set expectations with the interviewee, and decide if they will take notes through a tape recorder, on a laptop computer, or by filling in a protocol. Similarly, after the interview, students learn that they need to review their notes, add missing information, write a brief thank-you note, and make the appropriate citation.

Susan, in Indianapolis, planned specific mini-lessons to hone her students' skills in asking interview questions that require more than a "yes" or "no" response and keeping the interviewee on track. She began one minilesson by explaining:

> For our upcoming I-Search Unit on natural disasters, you will be interviewing a person who is an expert or who has valuable experience to share. Don't worry. If you need help in locating a person to interview, I'll be happy to help you. After you have contacted the person to set the time and date, you'll need to prepare by writing five interview questions. Let's talk about what makes a good question. Who's willing to volunteer to play the role of the interviewer while I play the role of the expert being interviewed?

When Andrea raised her hand to volunteer, Susan handed her two index cards with questions. They sat down facing each other in front of the class. Andrea asked the first question from the first index card, "Have you ever been in a blizzard?" Susan responded, "Yes."

Susan then turned to the class and asked them for their reaction to this question. One student responded that Andrea asked a question for which she already knew the answer. Andrea then asked the next question, "Do you remember any of the effects?" Susan's only response was a nod of her head. Reverting back to her role as teacher, Susan made a critical point:

> You don't want to ask a "skinny" question because then you'll get a "skinny" answer. When Andrea asked me the question, 'Do you remember any of the effects?' my answer was something she probably already knew because that's why she had chosen me for her interview. How could she reword the question to get a more elaborate answer?"

As the students offered the following alternatives, Susan recorded their suggestions:

- Could you tell me some of the effects?
- Explain the emotions you felt being in the blizzard.

Another student commented that the second question sounded more like a command. Susan agreed and suggested that they might want to rephrase it. However, she added, that asking for an explanation was a good tactic. Susan then asked the class, "What other words could we use to begin a question to get an answer that yields good information?"

Students responded with, "Why?" "What?" "When?" "Where?" and "How?" Susan ended the lesson by explaining that the next day they would practice posing questions with a partner. She reminded them that they wanted to ask questions that would help them find out information they did not already know.

For their I-Search Unit on social activism, the teachers in Lawrence, New York, required every student to conduct a relevant interview. To double-check the relevancy factor, teachers asked students to explain why they had chosen that particular individual to interview. For example, one student, who interviewed George Andrews of the New York office of the FBI for his search on terrorism, explained that Mr. Andrews "knew a lot about specific terrorists, criteria for identifying someone as a terrorist, and how to handle threatening notes written by terrorists." The teachers also reviewed the students' questions beforehand to make sure that they were productive and would yield good information. Questions such as these for Mr. Andrews were deemed satisfactory:

- What do you think is the most popular characteristic in a terrorist that makes them want to kill people?
- How do you distinguish between a terrorist, a serial killer, a murderer, and an assassin?
- What do terrorists usually want out of killing people?

Figure 3.3 lists the names or occupations of other people interviewed by students in this class and gives a sample of interview questions.

Teachers Help Students Apply Skills.
Once teachers feel that students have developed a set of rudimentary skills, they find meaningful ways for students to apply these skills. A mini-I-Search, usually lasting from two days to a week, is a good way to address the young adolescents' need to gradually acquire fluency in using newly acquired research skills in a meaningful context.

For example, in Indianapolis, Susan, the 7th grade language arts teacher, and her teammate Ann, the social studies teacher, designed a mini-unit as an outgrowth of a short newspaper unit. After students selected one newspaper article they found particularly intriguing, they posed a narrowly defined question to explore further. The students developed a focused plan to gather resources, went to the library, and prepared an oral mini-exhibition. At the end of the unit, students reflected on the experience by responding to the question, "What did I learn about library research?" One student related what she learned:

I learned how to use microfilms. Microfilms are films of newspapers and magazines. I learned how to find exactly what you're looking for, using Infotrac. Infotrac is a computer that can draw you to find what you're looking for.

When Susan, Ann, and the rest of the team implemented the full-blown I-Search Unit the next semester, their expectations came to fruition. Students felt secure in applying a repertoire of newly acquired research skills.

During Phase I

Teachers use the *read, watch, ask,* and *do* rubric to guide their own design of Phase I immersion activities, as described in the previous chapter. They reason that if they expect students to understand the value of using diverse materials and resources, then they should model how this can be done outside of the library walls. At the close of Phase I, many teachers plan an activity to help students reflect on the materials and resources used during immersion. When teachers make transparent what might have been opaque, young adolescents are better able to understand expectations. Young adolescents respond favorably when they see that their teachers expect the same from themselves as they do from students.

Teachers often create a chart on a bulletin board with four columns labeled *read, watch, ask,* and *do.* As they review the Phase I activities, teachers and students list the immersion materials and resources under the appropriate heading.

FIGURE 3.3
Selected Interviews by Students in Lawrence

Topic	Person Interviewed	Sample Question
Immigration	Dennis Martin, handles immigration in local Councilman's office	What are the views of Americans on legal immigration into the United States?
Oil Spills and Animals	Ed Sorenson, President of Ecowater Systems	Which animals are most affected by oil spills and why?
Gun Control	Anonymous NRA public relations person	Why is there a debate over gun control?
The Exxon-Valdez Oil Spill	Bruce A. Wriget, National Marine Fisheries Service	What are the cleanup efforts from the Exxon-Valdez oil spill?
Child Abuse	Person at the Child Abuse Hotline in Idaho	Why does child abuse happen and what can be done to break the cycle?
Cults	Representative from the AFF, the international cult education program	Why and how do cults grow?

One positive outcome of this activity is that students can later draw on these materials if needed for their own searches. As Lynda from Bedford said, "They can feel as if they have already started their research." For young adolescents who may have difficulty in getting started, this initial boost is welcomed.

During Phase II

A search plan serves as a blueprint for carrying out the research. Having a plan in hand gives young adolescents a sense of security as they ready themselves for the next phase of their search. Teachers tell students that although the search plan they develop in Phase II will certainly be modified when they engage in their search in Phase III, having a plan serves as a starting point. Students agree that this strategy serves to prevent later frustration. As one student in Indianapolis commented, "I think the plan is going to help us get our information. It's going to be definitely worth the time we take."

Before students develop their plans, they need time to browse through materials. Browsing can take place in the classroom, the school library, the town or city library, or even a college or university library. For example, students in Bedford began browsing for information by delving into materials already collected by teachers and the librarian during curriculum design.

Teachers had copied newspaper and magazine articles, in addition to book chapters. They organized these, along with videos, on a rolling cart that students wheeled from one classroom to another. For further browsing, students went to the school library, where Joan had created a special area with materials collected from the elementary school, the high school, and the town library.

The two basic components of a search plan answer the questions "What resources?" and "In what order should the resources be accessed?"

What Resources to Access. Teachers want students to be as specific as possible in developing the "what" component of the plan. For example, one student was planning to make some telephone calls to find information for her question, "How does Georges Bank affect the New England economy and the fishing industry?" Marcia, her teacher, encouraged her to begin collecting the telephone numbers so there would be no hurdles to overcome later.

Teachers have found that tools can help students organize the "what" part of the plan. One simple tool used frequently by teachers consists of a handout of four sheets of paper as shown in Figure 3.4 (see next page). The headings on each sheet are "Read," "Watch," "Ask," and "Do," as modeled during the immersion period. Here, students can list the potential resources they find during browsing.

Teachers in Bedford used the *Search Organizer* in Phase II because the software allowed students to record the author and title, identify where the resource could be found, and enter a full citation with the help of an online guide (Figure 3.5, on p. 50). Later, when students were

going on their searches, they printed the list of resources to take to the library.

In What Order to Access Resources. The second component of the plan asks students to explain, "In what order do you plan to access the materials and resources?" Sequence is important for building and constructing knowledge. Teachers want students to understand that gathering information from different sources is not a haphazard process. As students gather information, they are constructing knowledge. New knowledge creates the context for the next information being sought. Therefore, students need to take into account how one resource will inform or enhance the next.

Some teachers ask students to use a calendar to plan the sequence of their searches. As Ann, in Indianapolis, passed out a blank calendar for the upcoming month, she explained:

> As you fill out this calendar, think about a logical order for delving into the materials. For example, one approach might be to first gather general information. Even the encyclopedia and other reference materials such as an atlas play a role here. This can provide a good general knowledge base from which to launch into other, more specific materials.

When Ann's students began filling in the calendars, she noted that Julian developed a sequence that began with first watching a videotape and then reading a book. Knowing how this student processed information, the teacher asked, "Would it help you to learn more by beginning with the more general text first, and then moving to the more specific video?"

FIGURE 3.4
Tool to Help Students Develop Search Plan

DO

GATHERING INFORMATION—DO

Examples: Computer simulation; field trip; experiment; game

ASK

GATHERING INFORMATION—ASK

Examples: Interview; questions; survey; network

WATCH

GATHERING INFORMATION—WATCH

Examples: Video; television show; CD-ROM; slides; filmstrips

READ

GATHERING INFORMATION—READ

Examples: Fiction; nonfiction; newspaper; magazine; pamphlet; encyclopedia; database; downloaded materials from the Internet

FIGURE 3.5
Screens from *Search Organizer* to Help Students Develop Search Plan

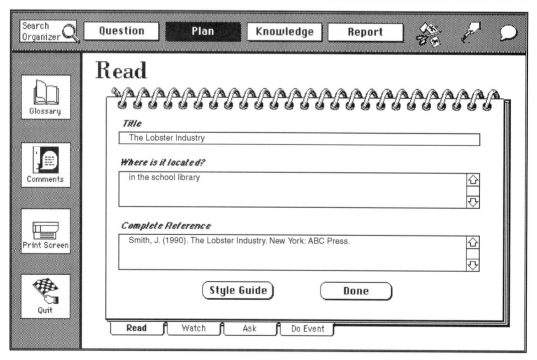

After thinking about the question, Julian decided to first skim the text; second, watch the video; and, third, return to the text to reread it more closely. In contrast, in another case, the teacher knew that the student was a visual learner and would benefit from first watching a video to develop images that would give meaning to other information.

Students can draft their search plans in many formats. Some teachers accept outlines, filled-in versions of the tools, or calendars. Other teachers ask students to write their search plan in a narrative form, as in the following example:

> My plan is to go to an encyclopedia first; they provide general information and usually are a good place to start. Then I plan to look in the school library for books on whaling and to check the National Geographic index to see if there are any articles on whaling. I plan to use SIRS in the computer room to find more magazine articles. Another idea I am toying with is to use the Internet to find information, maybe see what Greenpeace has to say about whaling. I know where to go for my *do* section, New Bedford. I know there is a museum there, and I also know it is an important port because of a line in an old whaling song I know, "They send you to New Bedford town, that famous whaling port." For my *watch,* I plan on looking for a National Geographic documentary and maybe a video of Moby Dick. For the *ask,* I plan on writing the whaling museum on Nantucket and seeing if I can do a telephone interview as a follow-up.

Teachers review the emerging search plans, assessing them against the students' questions, learning style, and mandated criteria. With feedback from teachers, students revise their search plans to make them more complete and diverse before teachers sign off.

During Phase III

During Phase III (gathering and integrating information), teachers can support students' searches in three ways: help students access resources, assess difficulties, and encourage students to revise search plans so that they are working for and not against the student.

Teachers Help Students Access Resources. Teachers make arrangements, help students share resources, and solicit parental and community support. Though many young adolescents relish the opportunity to actively search for information, the majority need the security of knowing that they will have access to resources at regularly scheduled times. To assuage student fears, many teachers take responsibility for making arrangements. They create a Phase III schedule for going to a library (school library, town library, and college or university library). Teachers in interdisciplinary teams often set up a rotating schedule (see Figure 3.6, p. 52). For example, Monday is the day that the language arts teacher takes every class to the library. On Tuesday, it is the science teacher's turn. This way, students go to the library one period each day, but with a different teacher each day.

As Phase III was about to begin in Bedford, Joan, the librarian, met with the teachers to share with them what she had learned over the years about making library time as useful as possible for students. She explained that teachers need to be engaged in supervision, checking in with the students to ask what they found, what they need,

FIGURE 3.6
Rotating Schedule During Phase III

Subject	Monday	Tuesday	Wednesday	Thursday	Friday
Language Arts	Take all classes to library				Take all classes to library
Science		Take all classes to library			
Mathematics			Take all classes to library		
Social Studies				Take all classes to library	

and what the possible next steps should be. For those times when the whole class comes to the library, teachers need to set up varied activities to address the common problem of too many students, too little teacher and librarian help, and too few resources. A possible solution is for students to come to the library in small groups of three for only 15–20 minutes at a time. Once students find what they need, they can then photocopy it or check it out.

Some teachers also make arrangements for students to conduct interviews during the school day. This responds to a need voiced by one student in California: "Many children do not have a clue as to where to find someone to interview." To meet this need for their students in Indianapolis, Susan and Ann invited several different speakers to school on a particular day during Phase III of their I-Search Unit on Water Pollution and Conservation. Students had the option to sign up

to interview relevant speakers throughout the day. One interview with Jeff Keely, from the Environmental Protection Agency in Washington, D.C., transpired via the telephone. Having rehearsed the day before, students efficiently took turns on the speakerphone as others took notes.

Teachers create organized opportunities for students to share information, give one another feedback, and affirm what others are doing. Teachers can build on the young adolescents' need for social interaction by having students learn to help each other to locate information. For example, one student in Indianapolis explains a peer-helping strategy that Susan and Ann developed:

> We had these certificates that you fill out. . . . You put down the name of the person who helped you. You write how they helped you and the date they

helped you, and you write your signature on the dotted line. It can't be something like putting a book on a shelf. It has to be like finding information and giving it to them. There is a big box for putting the certificates in. Later, our name might be chosen to receive a prize.

The Bedford team used two "Help Thy Neighbor" strategies:

• Teachers created a help board in the hallway where students could use Post-it notes to ask for help in locating a resource. A potential helper took down the note and sought out the student in need.

• Teachers organized an hourlong, teamwide help session in the cafeteria. Students with similar questions met together in small groups. Everyone came armed with his or her favorite or most useful resources. Then, when someone asked for help, another student could not only make a recommendation but also place a resource into thankful, outstretched hands.

Many teachers expect that students will continue their investigative legwork after school and on the weekends. This might be the only way a student can watch a television show, visit a business or industry, interview a relative, or do a survey in his or her neighborhood. This aspect of the search requires parental and community support, which teachers often elicit before the unit begins. Teachers have found that sending letters home to parents before the unit starts, placing articles in school newsletters, and posting notices in public libraries builds awareness and garners support.

Teachers Assess Students' Progress.

Young adolescents often feel embarrassed to ask

for help, thinking it shows their vulnerability. Having accepted the responsibility of the search, they might be afraid to reveal that they are not succeeding. When students are trying to protect themselves in this way, teachers must determine what is or is not working well through ongoing assessment strategies. After identifying a problem, many teachers intervene to give students a needed boost—for example, helping with phone calls, locating additional resources, or writing letters.

Teacher strategies for this kind of ongoing assessment include asking students a set of questions that they can answer conversationally or in writing. Questions such as the following can ferret out problems:

• What are three good things that have happened so far during your research? Why were they good?

• What problems are you having? Explain how you intend to solve them.

• What is missing from your research so far, either in terms of information or ways to find it?

Teachers also review student journals, with student permission, as a way to assess student needs. Figure 3.7 (see next page) presents the journal entries one student made over a few days. These three entries reveal the student's frustration and provided the teacher with a window into the student's search. Based on this information, the teacher was able to develop a set of strategies to help this student find productive avenues for gathering information.

Teachers Encourage Students to Revise Search Plans. Revision of the search plan in Phase III is expected. Not only do students shift

---

FIGURE 3.7
Sample from Student Journal That Helped Teacher Assess Need for Help

---

March 29th and 30th

. . . I called a number for a law enforcement agency. The secretary that picked up said to call back the next day and ask for someone else. The secretary said that this person could help find the information I was looking for but that day was her day off (talk about bad timing). The next day, I called the number again and asked for the person. The secretary hooked me up to the person, but all I got was the answering machine.

April 11

I spent most of the time in the office making phone calls. In my group of common topics, someone gave me a number for a lobster hatchery. I went to the school office and called the number. The person that picked up was very nice and after I explained what I was looking for, he said that I should call another number to another law enforcement agency.

The person said, though, that he would send any information he had that I could use. Next I called the number the man at the hatchery said to call. The person that picked up told me to call another number to the Coast Guard. That person said that she would send me info that I could use. I called the Coast Guard next and they fixed me up with a captain who would help me answer some questions. They told me that the captain would call me at 3:00 p.m. on April 12th. The Coast Guard also gave me another phone number that went to the Department of Fisheries Wildlife Environmental Law Enforcement, which I had already called on March 29 and 30.

April 12th

At 3:00 p.m., I was waiting at the phone for half an hour waiting for the captain to call. The captain did not call and at 3:45 p.m., I gave up and called Douglas G. Marshall. Douglas is the exclusive director of a few meetings and discussions that were going on about new lobster laws. I called the number but he was not there.

direction as a result of teacher feedback, but they also revise their plans based on unfolding leads. The essence of the search is fluidity; being able to discover the unexpected and being prepared for breakthroughs.

For example, under the category of *read* in his search plan, a student in Bedford listed the book, "Lobsters: Gangsters of the Sea," an article from the magazine section of the Sunday newspaper, and another magazine article from a periodical on fishing. But once his search was under way, he found information in the *Boston Globe* describing lobstering in Maine. This led him to the *Bangor Daily News,* which, in turn, led him to two brochures from the Division of Law Enforcement (*1994 Massachusetts Lobster Status Report* and *Lobster and Crab Laws and Restrictions*). He also discovered a set of rules proposed at a public meeting from the New England Fishery Council, which he found by searching on Lexis Nexis. He might not have been able to unearth such valuable information unless he had started with an initial plan of action.

During Phase IV

In Phase IV, students prepare an I-Search Paper, an exhibition, or both. In Chapter 5, we describe in detail how students explain their search methodology (backed up by full citations in the references section), recount the high and low points of the search, and reflect on what they learned about themselves as active researchers. Teachers want students to review how and what they learned so that they can take charge of their learning now and in the future.

Final Comments

As young adolescents become engaged in their searches, they begin to recognize that they are taking responsibility for accessing information. As decision makers, they are in charge of their own inquiry.

Extremely important during this developmental stage, middle school students want to test their abilities to be independent, explore their worlds, move away from what is safe and familiar, and not follow the dictates of adults. By designing, carrying out, and modifying a search plan, they become accountable for determining what kinds of resources are most productive for their questions. By reflecting on this process, they develop a personal awareness of what transpired. One student reflected: "I noticed that I developed as a researcher when I started looking in resources other than books to find information."

The fundamental goal for accessing varied materials and resources is to construct knowledge. In the next chapter, we discuss the meaning-making process. What helps students carry out this essential task?

Making Meaning

After two weeks of searching for information about the animals that lived on or near the Amazon River, Michael was ready to do more sorting. He had already classified the animals into three categories: reptiles (e.g., tree cobras, pythons), mammals (chimpanzee, okapi), and amphibians (turtles, Suriname toad). Now, he was adding more animals to these categories—lizard and anaconda went under the reptile group; and poison frog and variegated toad fit under amphibians. His next step would be to list the characteristics of each animal. Later, he would create categories of characteristics in terms of physical appearance, habitat, and prey.

Michael is making meaningful connections, linking prior knowledge and experience to what he is learning. He is discovering patterns and discerning relationships that matter on a personal level. On the road to lifelong learning, he is like all of us, striving to develop deep understandings and comprehend phenomena.

Phase III of an I-Search Unit is purposely designed to help students make meaning over a sustained period of time. For about two to four weeks, students gather and analyze information, integrating it to formulate concepts. The goal is for students to actively process information, consolidating and internalizing it in a way that is both conceptually coherent and personally meaningful.

During the entire I-Search Unit, and particularly in Phase III, teachers provide students with varied experiences that enable them to perceive the patterns that connect ideas and develop concepts. Teachers can draw students' attention to essential concepts related to their questions and the overarching concepts of the unit.

Teachers can enhance student meaning making in many ways: introducing effective strategies for *extracting relevant information* from different sources; helping students to *perceive patterns and relationships* by analyzing and synthesizing information from their notes; and guiding students to develop gestalts.

Extracting Relevant Information

How does the student find the truly relevant information that is written in the book, contained in the video, uttered during an interview, posted in an Internet newsgroup, or contained within a Web site? How does the student isolate the kernels of information that most pointedly connect to his or her search? Further, how does the student record this information in his or her own words? Teachers use three strong instructional strategies to help students extract relevant information: They explicitly teach students to take notes, engage in peer conferences, and keep a glossary.

Taking Notes

One student's comment, "First, you have to know how to take notes," shows that we cannot assume that all students have acquired this skill. Susan, the language arts teacher in Indianapolis, found that her students were highlighting photocopies of books, magazines, and computer printouts of Internet messages and electronic encyclopedias as a substitute for note taking. To rectify the situation, she modeled the note-taking process, using her own search question about the uses of soybeans. As she demonstrated what she was doing, she provided the following running commentary:

> I locate a book that has some information that can help me. I keep my question in front of me at all times so that I know what it is that I am looking for (i.e., the uses of soybeans for the home). I immediately write down the name of the book and other pertinent information so that I have the reference. I use the table of contents and the index to find the parts of the book where relevant information might be found. Then I begin reading.
>
> When I find something useful, because it's related to my question, I place a yellow Post-it next to the section that seems to have the information I want. I will want to come back to this later. When I do return to these sections, I am ready to write down what I learned related to my question, in my own words.
>
> For example, I am writing that soybeans are legumes, and tofu is a soybean product that is soft and white and has a cheeselike quality. I make sure that I am writing this information in words I will understand. I am blending the words in the book with my own words. This is called paraphrasing. It's not just copying exactly what is in the book onto my notecard. By using my own words, I am showing myself that I understand what I have read.

Next, as Susan showed students how she took notes from the printout of an electronic version of the *World Book Encyclopedia*, she continued her commentary:

> I read through this printout and find information that's related to my question.

. . . I use my highlighter pen to underline only the information about how soybeans are used in the home. Then, I reread all of the highlighted text. I am focusing on how the soybean is used in products in the home. I take notes from what was highlighted. Once again, I use my own words in conjunction with words from the printout. I don't write anything that doesn't answer my question. For example, I'm not going to write anything about what the plant looks like . . . [or] how the soybean is used to make fuel.

Susan then gave her students time for note taking. As students were working independently, she checked in with each one to see if he or she was able to extract relevant information and paraphrase these ideas. If students had difficulty, she asked them to stop and just tell her what was important. As students spoke, Susan's transcription became their "notes." One student, LaShana, had an "aha" experience:

When you copy out of a book, you're wasting time. You really give yourself more work to do. If you copied exactly what was in the book, you would still need to put it in your own words. So that's why you are wasting time.

As their students' piles of notecards grew, the teachers in Bedford asked students to pause, review their notes, extract relevant information, and input this distilled information into the *Search Organizer* software. For example, as Matt reviewed his notes, he chose a few key ideas to input into the *Search Organizer,* as shown in Figure 4.1. For Matt and many other students who are still thinking concretely, reviewing notes, deciding what's relevant, and keeping a running

list of this information on the computer (even a word processing file will do) is a supportive basic strategy that contributes to later analysis.

Participating in Peer Conferences

Peer conferencing is an excellent strategy for helping students extract relevant information. It invites active involvement around the exchange of ideas and compels students to put into words ideas that may still be a bit unclear in their minds (Harmin, 1994). Working together in pairs, students can stimulate each other to make sense of what they are learning. Peer conferencing meets young adolescents' basic needs for social contact and freedom of expression. The strategy builds on their interpersonal intelligence, defined as the ability to listen and express ideas to others (Gardner, 1983).

A good example comes from Indianapolis where two boys worked together as an investigative team during a unit on disasters. Their question was, "What caused the *Titanic* to sink?" After both read the same book, they watched a documentary. Their social studies teacher, Ann, encouraged them to discuss what they were learning. Here is part of their conversation:

Student 1: I thought it was pretty interesting that they knew the iceberg was coming but they didn't do anything about it until they realized it would be a threat and sink their ship. And when they finally tried to do something, it was too late. They tried to turn and they ran into the side of it. If they had hit it head-on, they probably wouldn't have sunk. I need to find out why.

Student 2: They said that if they pulled the boat over four more inches, they would have missed it.

FIGURE 4.1
Note Taking Using the *Search Organizer*

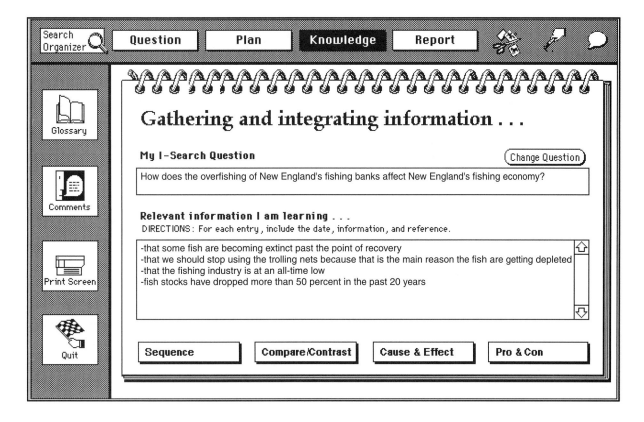

Student 1: They said it wasn't the iceberg that really caused the big hole in the Titanic. They said it was the pressure from the water and the iceberg that caused a little leak and made it pop. It started sinking.

This conversation served as a precursor to having each student record a relevant set of notes in his own words.

Creating Glossaries

Keeping a glossary is a form of note taking that helps students extract relevant ideas.

Teachers encourage students to keep a running list of words and phrases that capture key terminology related to their search. They ask students to enter definitions that are in their own words, explanations, and examples. On the surface, the glossary appears to be an unsophisticated strategy, but it offers powerful benefits. A thorough knowledge and fluency with words related to a specific area are a prerequisite for making meaning. A Chinese proverb says, "The beginning of wisdom is to call things by their right names."

Some teachers realize that a lack of understanding of words and phrases related to a new content area can create a barrier for students. That's why the glossary has stood the test of time. It helps students understand and apply vocabulary words and terms appropriately.

For example, a student in Lawrence participating in a unit on social activism was doing a search on sexism in the workplace. Drawing on words from her glossary (e.g., *discrimination, glass ceiling, harassment, rape, sexism, society,* and *Title IX*), she spoke with authority in class discussions and used these words when she conducted interviews. She later included appropriate terminology in her I-Search paper.

Many teachers draw on technology applications to help students create glossaries. The computer makes it easier to re-alphabetize entries and gives students the freedom to expand or revise their definitions. Some teachers rely on the glossary feature included in the *Search Organizer* software because it has these features.

Perceiving Patterns and Relationships

Making meaning, or forming a gestalt, relies on students' organizing their information into patterns, or mental maps. When students form patterns, they break down larger pieces of information into smaller pieces and then rearrange the smaller pieces so that they interlock in meaningful ways. This reformulation into a thoughtful whole is at the heart of meaning making (Caine & Caine, 1991). Until information finds a "home" in a meaningful pattern, learners can feel uneasy or agitated. Teachers have an important role to play in helping students to perceive patterns and relationships: They teach strategies

that separate the wheat from the chaff, and they introduce visual tools and graphic organizers.

Strategies for Separating the Wheat from the Chaff

Caught up in a blitz of note taking, students proudly display their ever-growing stack of notecards. But students need to go beyond having a physical pack of notecards to actually making meaning. It takes active processing for students to make sense of the information they are gathering. Therefore, the next step involves sorting through the growing number of notes to separate the relevant notes from those that are less critical. As one student explained to a classmate, "You want to pick out the really important stuff."

Sorting requires students to make decisions about what is and is not important. The criteria for these decisions change over time as a function of a student's growing knowledge base. The following axiom applies: "The more you understand, the better able you are to evaluate what is important or relevant." As students collect more information, they usually become more focused. What might have been deemed unimportant at the early stages of a search can prove to be significant when linked to other information gleaned at a later stage. The reverse is also possible; what seemed like a critical piece of information at an earlier stage may lose its importance when viewed against other information.

Marilyn, a teacher in Bedford, suggested a helpful strategy: she asked students to review their notes periodically. Following Marilyn's suggestion, one student explained what she did:

> I had a whole mess of notes, but I
> had to actually go through them. I just

read each and every single thing I found. So I realized that just because you have a lot of information doesn't mean you have information you actually want. As I read through all of them, I realized that there are a lot of things I don't need and a lot of things I do need.

What makes students need some but not other information is that the information rounds out an idea, justifies a point, or clarifies an issue. These are all aspects of meaning making. Without this information, the full picture would be incomplete. In contrast, information that can be discarded is irrelevant, distracting, or out of sync with the emerging concept.

Using Marilyn's recommended strategy, one student made two color-coded piles to represent relevant and irrelevant information. He didn't want to throw anything out because notes deemed unimportant at this stage might change to a more valued status later as relationships among ideas became clearer. Once the student reviewed his notes, Marilyn encouraged him to sort items into categories he defined for himself. This strategy supported the student's ability to impose meaning on available information.

Jennifer, another Bedford student, met with Lynda, the language arts teacher, to review her large set of notes about the rise and fall of the whaling industry in Nantucket. Lynda's goal was to help Jennifer see that there were multiple ways to sort this information depending on what was contained in the notes and what Jennifer wanted to focus on. For example, as they both read through the notes, it became apparent that the names of different occupations related to whaling were interspersed throughout the notes. Lynda suggested that one cut into Jennifer's

information would be to cull all of the occupations. Jennifer, warming to the concreteness of this task, began her list:

> Blacksmiths—supply the harpoons and other whalecraft of the industry
> Brokers and merchants—finance and insure the whaling voyages
> Coopers—provide the barrels needed on the voyage
> Masons—build the tryworks (furnace to render oil from blubber) on the deck of a whaler
> Oil refiners—purify the main product of the island, the whale oil

The next day, Jennifer and Lynda met again. This time, Lynda suggested that they apply a different lens to review the notes. Referring back to Jennifer's question about the rise and fall of whaling, Lynda asked Jennifer to suggest another perspective. This time Jennifer replied, "I have a lot of notes about different time periods. Let me sort my information that way." A chronological analysis proved to be a helpful next step. After sorting cards into piles that represented decades, Jennifer then went to the computer to begin drafting some paragraphs:

> During the years between 1600 and 1720, whaling was first attempted on the island by the original purchasers. The long-continued practice of the industry provided Nantucket with a great dexterity in the business. Indians were employed on the vessels due to their adaptability. Nantucket whalers hunted mainly sperm whales.
> During the 1720 to 1820 whaling era, the European countries were all burning more oil, so Boston had a higher demand for it. However, there was a

bounty on all whaling vessels of 20 shillings per ton, so although there was a high demand for Nantucket's product, the islanders were having a lot more trouble supplying it. Also, by 1726 the ending point of shore whaling was reached, so massive progress was made in the art of whaling by the 1800's.

By 1870, the end of the whaling business was hitting Nantucket hard. The loss of whales was killing the island; there was a loss of money and a loss of hope. They thought that fishing for cod might be the new industry for the island; however, the islanders didn't adapt and the cod idea failed them. However, the loss of these industries brought a new hope, tourism. Fine old houses were being bought and turned into hotels. Siasconset was one of the island's three towns. It was a farming and fishing town and suddenly it was turned into a tourist haven. A ferry line was set up between Nantucket and Woods Hole, and a train line between Woods Hole and Boston.

Later, as Jennifer gathered more information, she further revised her drafts. She learned a valuable lesson: Sorting information is an iterative task; a single analysis is never enough.

The sorting process serves as a means of assessment for both teachers and students. As teachers review students' work, they can see how far students have progressed in note taking, whether they are using strategies for extracting information and whether they are beginning to link information and create usable categories. An analysis of this information can help teachers plan more focused or individualized strategies to help students who need additional support. Self-assessment helps students reflect on their research process.

One student in New York, taking notes on AIDS, said, "I had so much information that I didn't need and so little information that I did need." The very fact that she realized that some information was more valuable than other information indicates that she was making meaning. Her self-appraisal of the situation also helped her set goals and redirect her information-gathering efforts.

A team of teachers in Long Beach, California, talked about particular students who they expected might have difficulty letting go of information. The teachers anticipated that these students would argue, "I've done all this work. I've accumulated all these notecards. Now, you tell me I can't use them!" Therefore, before the students could utter even one word of complaint, the teachers made a preemptive strike at the beginning of Phase III. They explained:

> Our role is to help you learn how to think. Your ability to sort your cards, to recognize what is important and what is not important, shows how good a thinker you are. In fact, we want you to hold aside and show us all of the notecards you are not using. Not only do we value what you have included; we value what you have not included.

This explanation not only satisfied the students, but also motivated them. Teachers gave students credit for "extra" notes placed in an appendix at the end of the I-Search paper.

Strategies Involving Visual Tools and Graphic Organizers

Teachers recognize that for some students, thinking with images is more useful than thinking verbally. These students can better express ideas and more easily perceive patterns through pictures, maps, diagrams, charts, and webs. The use of visual tools respects multiple intelligences (Gardner, 1993), particularly spatial intelligence, where students are able to perceive the visual-spatial world and make transformations on those perceptions. Graphic organizers are one class of visual tools that teachers can introduce to students to help them manage and display information. The tools rely on a student's ability to generate and manipulate visual images.

Visual tools can play an important role in fostering students' deep content learning (Hyerle, 1996). They help students analyze and synthesize information by organizing it into something that makes sense, breaking it down into separate parts, and then reformulating it into something coherent. As Hyerle says, graphic organizers can help students comprehend, delineate, summarize, and synthesize ideas found in different sources. Some of these graphics can be highly formalized, and teachers can generate them to fit a specific content-learning process. Others can be created by students in response to a particular exploration.

Concept maps or webs are one of the most common graphic organizers. They are attractive to students who feel constrained by the linear nature of text and need to use arrows to connect ideas organized within space. One student in Bedford used the software program *Inspiration* (1992) to create a graphic organizer that

categorized what he was learning about the restrictions and laws related to lobstering (see Figure 4.2, on the next page). For this web, he used different geometric shapes as a concrete way to organize information into categories.

Another popular graphic organizer is the Venn diagram, useful for categorizing, as well as for comparing similar and different qualities of things (Hyerle, 1996). Young adolescents are attracted to this tool because of the elegance of the two overlapping circles. In the overlapping space, students can note what is the same about two items being compared. In the two nonoverlapping parts of the circle, they can identify what is unique about each item. Students in Indianapolis liberally used Venn diagrams in their I-Search Unit called, "A River Runs Through It." In studying different rivers around the world, they compared those rivers with the White River that courses through their own city. Figure 4.3 (on p. 65) represents one student's Venn diagram.

Timelines have wide appeal to young adolescents who like seeing a series of related events fall into place chronologically. Figure 4.4 (see p. 66) represents one Indianapolis student's day-by-day chronicling of the events related to the Galveston Flood of 1900. The timeline helped her visualize the devastation that occurred in a relatively short time. Technology-generated timelines (e.g., *Timeliner*, by Tom Snyder Productions, 1994) are particularly useful, allowing students to easily add or delete details.

In addition to webs, Venn diagrams, and timelines, many teachers have introduced other graphic organizers, on and off the computer, to help students analyze information. For example, the *Search Organizer* provides four ready-made

FIGURE 4.2
Use of *Inspiration* to Organize Notes into Categories

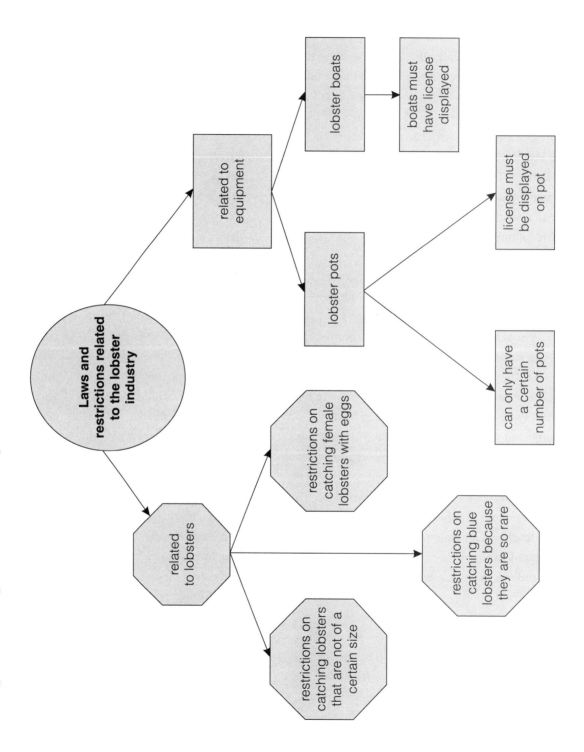

FIGURE 4.3
Sample of Student's Venn Diagram

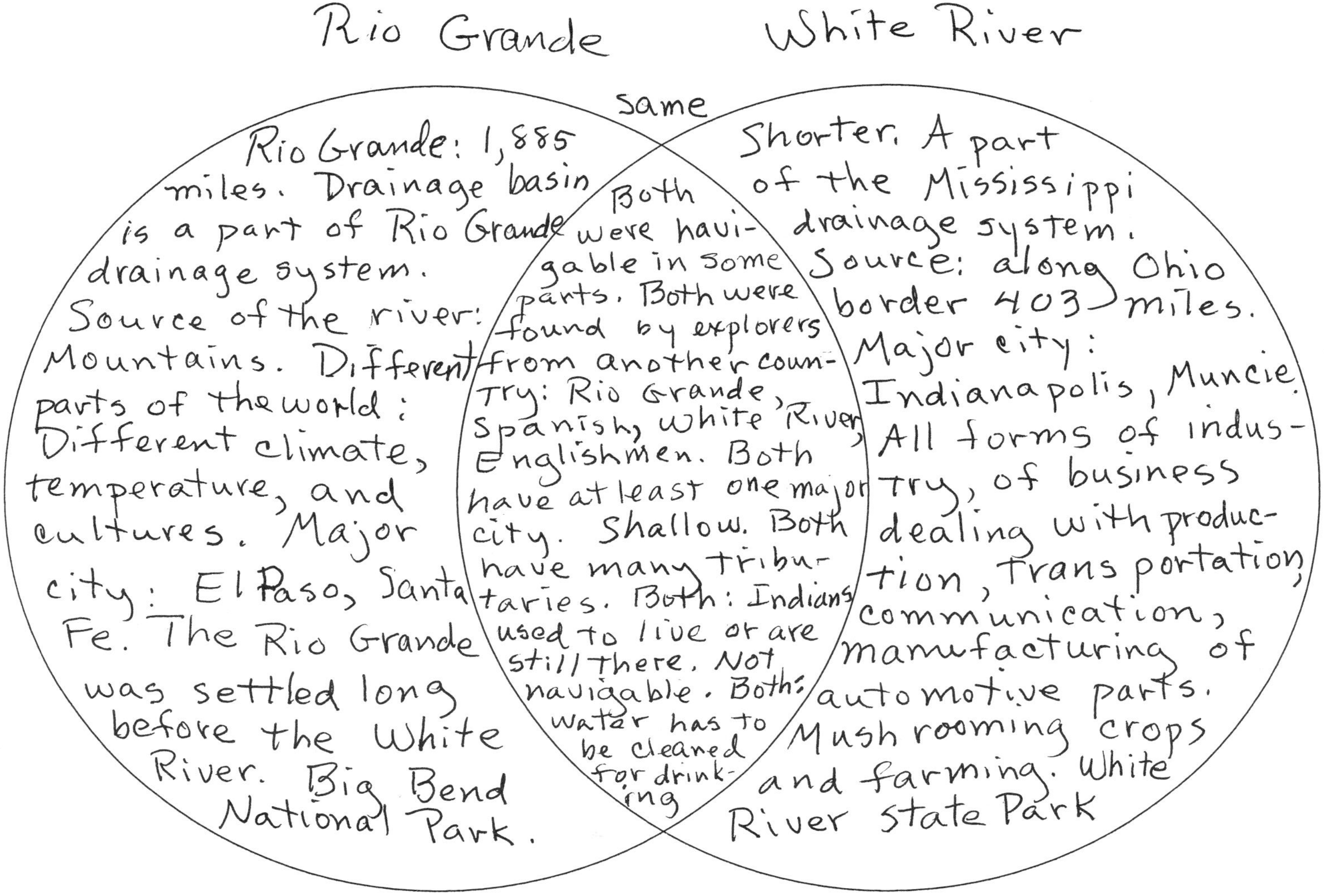

Rio Grande   Same   White River

Rio Grande: 1,885 miles. Drainage basin is a part of Rio Grande drainage system. Source of the river: found in Rocky Mountains. Different parts of the world: Different climate, temperature, and cultures. Major city: El Paso, Santa Fe. The Rio Grande was settled long before the White River. Big Bend National Park.

Both were navigable in some parts. Both were found by explorers. Different from another country: Rio Grande, Spanish, White River, Englishmen. Both have at least one major city. Shallow. Both have many tributaries. Both: Indians used to live or are still there. Not navigable. Both: water has to be cleaned for drinking

Shorter. A part of the Mississippi drainage system. Source: along Ohio border 403 miles. Major city: Indianapolis, Muncie. All forms of industry, All forms of business dealing with production, transportation, communication, manufacturing of automotive parts. Mushrooming crops and farming. White River State Park

---

FIGURE 4.4
Sample of Student Timeline

TIMELINE OF GALVESTON FLOOD
SEPTEMBER 8 – SEPTEMBER 14, 1900

Great Galveston Flood. Water 9 ft. deep in streets	Disaster discovered. Hundreds dead, thousands injured. Cry for help not yet realized	Deaths— 2,600, 4,000 houses ruined. Lower portion of city under water	Thousands of corpses found. Number of dead may reach 10,000	Theives begin to invade city, foraging through corpses + debris to find valuables	Property loss $ 20 million. Attempts to bury dead abandoned. Too many bodies	First real attempt to clean up debris piled along beach. Thousands dead
Sept. 8	Sept. 9	Sept. 10	Sept. 11	Sept. 12	Sept. 13	Sept. 14

---

templates (cause and effect, similarities and differences, pro and con, and sequence; see Figure 4.5). A teacher and student can decide if one or more template is relevant for meaning making based on the student's question and the kind of information being found. The use of any tool to help students analyze information aids in the development of gestalts.

Developing Gestalts

When students perceive a meaningful coming together of parts into patterns, they are developing a gestalt. Knowledge becomes almost like second nature because it is intricately meshed with what students already know (Caine & Caine, 1991). These patterns (tightly woven interconnections) are what we call *mental maps*. Mental maps are the abstractions that we derive by

relating past information to new information. However, we do not develop these mental maps, or abstractions, based solely on objective information. Rather, our emotional state (what we care about and react to) plays a key role in the development of gestalts. What we care about is what arouses our passion in learning; it drives and governs our sense of purpose. Our meaning making is influenced and organized by emotions and mind-sets based on expectancy (Caine & Caine, 1991).

To truly understand and know something is to care about it, and the more we care about a subject, the more we want to know. This spiraling eagerness serves to propel students forward in their searches and reinforces the development of gestalts. In the following mini-case studies, we trace the interplay between cognition and emotion for four students—Desray, Lori, Emily, and Melissa.

FIGURE 4.5
Templates in the *Search Organizer*

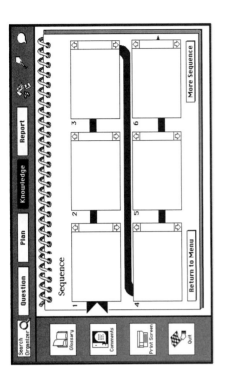

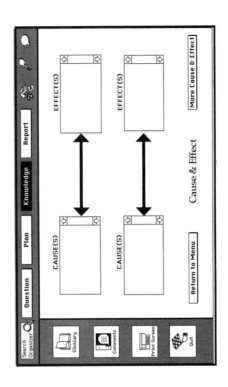

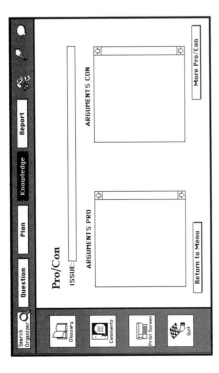

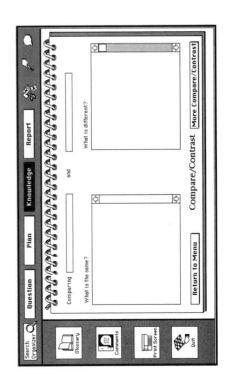

Mini-Case Studies

What is particularly interesting about these case studies is that all four students became concerned with moral and ethical issues. Typical of young adolescents, the students seemed to be asking themselves, "What does it all mean?" As part of the meaning-making process, they were evaluating information against a set of criteria. These criteria were based on their consciously or unconsciously held values and principles.

Desray's Personal Involvement. Desray's class in Indianapolis was engaged in a unit on disasters. The overarching concepts focused on what caused particular disasters, how disasters can be prevented or prepared for, and what the implications of disasters are.

Desray chose to explore the Central Soya Explosion, which occurred the year before on June 28, 1994, a mile from her house. Although this disaster probably did not make the national news, on a local level the explosion qualified as a traumatic event in Desray's life. She relates:

> Nothing had ever happened like this in our city. Some of my friends were in involved, and it was close to our home. My brother worked right near there, and I wanted to make sure that he wasn't in any danger that night. Plus people lost their homes because they burned up, and I feel sorry for them.

Desray had been home at the time of the explosion, just dozing off in her bed and listening to her Walkman. When the explosion erupted around midnight, Desray "could feel it and hear it." Jumping up to look out the window, she could "see something like a great big orange cloud over the western part of the sky." She and her family had to evacuate. Because of this personal involvement, Desray was motivated to gather information to make sense of this experience.

Desray, with the coaching of her teacher, started her search by reading a primary source— a police report given to her by her brother. He was privy to this information because he was one of the eyewitnesses interviewed by the police. The police report included his account of the explosion, descriptions by others, a summary by a police officer, and names of others involved. Desray drew a map to show what parts of the city were affected and where most of the people who were injured resided. She was already forming connections based on her knowledge of the area and what she was gleaning from other sources of information.

Desray checked the library to locate newspaper articles that described what caused the explosion and what the firefighters did when they arrived at the scene. From this, she learned the following:

> It was a chemical that had leaked from a barrel. Sensors weren't working in the yard, so it leaked into the street where people were walking. A man and his wife who were walking by could smell the chemicals. The man started running with his wife. Just then a car came along. A spark from the car ignited the chemicals, which caused the explosion. For two days afterward, a fire raged because the chemicals continued to leak.

Having established the cause of the explosion, Desray wanted to find out how the firemen stopped the leak and put the fire out. She also decided that she wanted to talk firsthand to people who had been involved in the event—and she had the police report with the names of all the eyewitnesses. Desray became engaged for the first time in her life in a planful investigation, driven by a need to know.

Desray also began to think about the implications of what she was learning in terms of the health of those nearby and the other environmental implications of the explosion. She knew that people were injured, but she wanted to find out about the long-term dangers of smoke inhalation: "The impact of the explosion was that the chemicals and the smoke got into the air and polluted it." The emotional connection motivating her investigation was becoming interwoven with developmentally appropriate concerns for ethical issues (e.g., where to build chemical plants).

Lori's Dilemma. Lori, a student in New York, participated in a unit on social action. Her I-Search question was, "What are the views of Americans on legal immigration into the United States?" As Lori gathered information, she had to ask herself about her own views on immigration. She recognized that her family had benefited from earlier proimmigration policies that allowed her great-great grandparents to enter the United States. But now she had a protectionist stance. She explained:

> But my current reason for limiting immigration is that this country already has enough problems and I feel that the recent flood of immigrants is adding to the problems in this country.

In gathering information, particularly by interviewing the councilman in her town, Lori began to question her own views. Her family had benefited from coming to America. Shouldn't others now also have the same opportunities? Once on the inside, is it right to deny to others what you had access to? This was not an easy moral question to answer.

Emily's Discovery. Emily, a student in Indianapolis, faced an issue different from Lori's. Emily was searching for information about the economic and social impact of the 1989 San Francisco Bay Area earthquake as part of her class's unit on disasters. She was taken aback by what she learned:

> It seems like with an earthquake like this, where so many people were affected, that most of the people would be driven to help other people. You know, by running to the hospital and helping out the injured or helping to prop up buildings that were falling. But when I was reading, the thing that I learned most about was that thousands of people were robbed because of the disadvantage they were at in not being able to protect themselves. Teenagers from housing developments rode the buses and roughed up passengers. And it just really surprised me because I was thinking it would be just the opposite. Everyone would be helping everyone else out because they all had the same experience—would know what it was like to go through the disaster. I was just surprised that people had lost so much already and they would lose even more when others stole their last possessions.

This information forced Emily to consider the code of ethics or behavior that guides human beings. She desperately wanted to believe that, within a society, people uphold basic laws, even when disaster strikes and the social order is in disarray. But that is not what she found. Given this particular example, Emily had to reconcile her beliefs with what she learned about the behavior of others. But beyond the life of the I-Search, Emily is certain to encounter many more examples, some of which will be consistent with what happened in San Francisco and others inconsistent. For Emily, this may be a gestalt that undergoes revision over time based on her life experiences.

Melissa's Empathy. Melissa, who also participated in the disasters unit in Indianapolis, was intrigued by the Galveston Flood of 1900. Melissa gathered a tremendous amount of information about floods in general and the Galveston Flood in particular. At the same time that Melissa was making sense of this factual information, she was also asking herself, "Why do I care?" Melissa's response to this age-old question reveals her belief system:

> Life is very important to me, and I believe it should be important to others. When I think of Galveston, I think of all the deaths and all the families and people that died. It's important to me that the people who died should be recognized.

Melissa's comment reflects the young adolescent's ability to connect personal concerns with social concerns (Beane, 1990). In her search for information about this disaster, she found herself thinking more deeply about the fragility of life. She realized that "you can't predict when a disaster or accident might be fatal." The possibility of the loss of life led her to think further about valuing people while they are alive, a deep and

fundamental thought about how we conduct our lives and interact with others. In personal terms, Melissa recognized that she should be concerned about how we "act toward other people" and why we should value friendship:

> I think we should all take the opportunity to make friends. Then we would have accomplished one of the best things in life (to have friends).

In Carol Gilligan's conceptual framework for moral development (1990), Melissa has adopted an ethic of care, viewing herself in terms of her relationship with others. This was a critical element of the gestalt she was forming.

Throughout Phase III, teachers use many of the same instructional strategies to help students develop gestalts as they have been using for extracting relevant information and forming patterns. Three specific strategies that teachers find effective are teacher-student conferences, peer conferences, and journal writing.

Holding Teacher-Student Conferences

Teachers' questions during teacher-student conferencing provide a scaffold for students. Within a safe environment, teachers push students to think more deeply, abstractly, or critically. Through gentle prodding, teachers can assist young adolescents to confront their assumptions and follow new paths of inquiry. In fact, during a successful teacher-student conference, the student realizes that the teacher is a collaborator with a shared goal—to make meaning.

Some teacher-student conferences occur informally or spontaneously. For example, one day in Bedford, Evan, who has learning disabilities, was in the school library. Evan's search centered on how the New England economy might be affected by the depletion of shellfish in the Atlantic Ocean. Seated in front of the computer, Evan was reading articles online from the *Boston Globe*. His teacher, circulating among the students, stopped at Evan's computer. He had just begun skimming an article on the Red Tide. Looking up from the screen, he asked his teacher, "Why is the Red Tide so important? Where is it located?"

The teacher praised him for generating these questions, explaining that when a reader asks questions, it helps focus the reading and enhance comprehension. She then suggested that Evan jot down his questions and keep reading to find out whether the article contained that information. Evan did so and made some notes.

The teacher waited nearby until he finished. She then asked him to summarize what he had learned. She asked him what his next step was going to be and how he was going to obtain more information.

Instead of answering immediately, Evan began writing something down. The teacher glanced down and saw that he had generated the following question: "What percentage of shellfish are toxic and how do you know?" Evan apologized for not answering immediately. He explained that the teacher's question had helped him link what he was reading to his next step, an interview with the manager of a seafood restaurant, and he hadn't wanted to lose that important thought. He said:

> I have been thinking that I have to know some things before I go to the restaurants. I have been thinking for a while about what I could be asking. This seems like a good question to put on my list.

Such impromptu teacher-student conferences are important, but many teachers schedule specific times to meet with students to discuss their progress as meaning makers. The give-and-take of these discussions often helps students clarify their ideas and perceive the kinds of connections that lead to forming gestalts. Teacher-student conversations can give students an opportunity to try out their new thinking about content. Teachers find that they can be most effective when they vary the kinds of questions they ask. For example, sometimes it is most appropriate to ask questions that elicit concrete responses. At other times, however, teachers find that by posing more complex questions, they are encouraging students to take risks in thinking abstractly and critically.

The following excerpt is from an information update in Bedford. By arrangement with his teacher, a student was summarizing what he had learned about the fishing industry. His teacher asked him questions to better understand the depth of his knowledge:

> *Teacher:* Let's talk about some of the information you've been gathering about the business end of the fishing industry.
>
> *Student:* Well, people kill fish to sell to restaurants. People get paid for the fish. However, when they are fishing, they are supposed to be throwing the little ones back. They are saying that there's not many big fish left, so that there are fewer fish to catch.
>
> *Teacher:* Why do they have to throw the little ones back?
>
> *Student:* So they can grow. Also, if they took all the little ones, all the big ones would die, since the big fish eat the little fish.

Even this brief exchange gives the teacher raw material to work with to encourage the student to think more deeply about content. For example, the teacher can tap into the student's prior knowledge about the food chain. Incorporating graphics, the student and the teacher can quickly sketch relationships—for example, which bigger fish eat which smaller fish. The teacher can then encourage the student to delve further into the exploration of restaurants, asking questions such as these: Do menus change depending on what kind of fish are plentiful during different seasons? How does this affect prices of fish purchased by the restaurant? How are these costs passed on to the consumer?

To answer these questions, the teacher and students can refer to the student's notecards; look over artifacts (e.g., restaurant menus); and inspect maps (e.g., a map of fishing areas in the Northeast). As they talk and point out interesting information to each other, they can each take separate notes. Later, the student can write a brief summary of the teacher-student conference, referring to his own notes, as well as the teacher's.

Arranging Peer Conferences

An exchange of ideas between two students who are both involved in a similar investigation can have positive benefits for both students as they see themselves as standing on common ground. As each student describes what he or she is learning, they echo each other's ideas. This give-and-take facilitates each student's ability to link ideas, perceive relationships, extend thoughts in new ways, and tap into dormant or inert ideas.

For example, here is an excerpt from two students' conversation in Bedford. Both focused on fishing.

Student 1: Without the Atlantic Ocean, New England's economy would be bad. I never really thought about it that way—how the Atlantic Ocean affects the economy. I thought about the Atlantic Ocean in relation to tourism and even how it affected different wars. But the Atlantic Ocean really has a big impact on New England.

Student 2: I really didn't know anything about the fishing industry. It's really teaching me a lot about that—we really have to take more care of our ocean and what we have left. We have really fragile space. We have to respect the animals that are still alive and the fish that spawn. We need to get the fishermen's jobs back. But the fishermen still shouldn't fish too much.

Student 1: I think I heard someplace that our [state] government is thinking of giving grants to fishermen to stop fishing. And for a few years, all the fish can come back. Like cod—they live 15 to 25 years but they spawn only every 7 years. I mean, we just have to let the fish come back. But if they did come back, then we might kill them again. But then when they come back, we have to save them.

Student 2: It really made me feel like, "Wow, what's gonna happen to us in 10 years? Are there going to be any fish left? Or are they all going to come back and it's going be like fish mania or something?" But if the fish do come back, I'd be so upset if the fishermen were just like, "Oh, fish" and they would do what they did before all over again.

They'd overfish again.

Student 1: It's made me think about what's going to happen in 10, 15, 20 years from now. I mean, where are we going to get our food if the fishing industry goes out? I mean, there's so much stuff that comes from it. Are we going to have fish farms next door where we can buy fish? I mean, what's there going to be? It really made me think about what's going to happen in the future.

These students hypothesized about the future together. They supported each other's genuine concerns, validating the social consciousness that develops in young adolescents. They also helped each other to think abstractly and form their own gestalt.

After a peer conversation is well under way, the teacher can check in with students to request a summary. This strategy helps students pause and reflect on the direction of the conversation. It also gives teachers an assessment point and an opportunity to redirect or expand the conversation. For example, the teacher might ask the two students conversing about overfishing to "retell" what they discussed, and then the teacher might try to enrich the conversation by asking questions about what could prevent overfishing.

Before they embark on peer conferences (as well as other strategies aimed at fostering meaning making), teachers and students should be clear about the goals, the way the experience is designed to meet those goals, and methods of determining whether the goals have been met. A set of guidelines developed jointly by teachers and students can help make peer conferencing a more productive enterprise. Here are some sample guidelines:

- *Students*. Which students would make the best peer conferencing partners? What factors should be considered to create balance (e.g., I-Search question, verbal ability, cognitive level, gender, communication style)?
- *Content*. What should be the focus of the conversation? How much structure should be placed on the conversation before it begins?
- *Conversational supports*. What will help students to be respectful listeners and effective conversationalists?
- *Materials*. What should students bring with them to the conversation to make it concrete (e.g., notes, portfolios, journals)?
- *Follow-up*. What follow-up in terms of notes will be expected?

Let's turn now to another strategy used throughout the search process journal writing— which also helps students develop gestalts.

Journal Writing

Journal writing usually begins in Phase I, but it gains importance in Phase III because it fosters *process mediation*. Writers hold an inner dialogue as a way of seeing another perspective and exploring the landscape of their own thoughts and feelings (Progoff, 1980).

A good example comes from Southern California, where students were engaged in a unit with the lively title of "California, Here We Come!" The overarching concepts focused on why people come to California, where they have come from, factors that affect their lives, and the impact of new settlers on those already living in California. Because many students were recent immigrants themselves, the response journal was a place for them to reflect on legal and illegal immigration, the implications of the state's Proposition 187, and proposed state and federal legislation related to immigration (all of which were hot topics in an upcoming election). Issues about border patrols and loss of health care for illegal immigrants were not abstractions to these students. The journal provided a safe place to ponder serious issues that aroused fear and anxiety.

Final Comments

Phase III of an I-Search unit is like doing a jigsaw puzzle, but harder. To begin a jigsaw, you open the box, spread out the pieces, study the picture on the cover of the box (which serves as a gestalt), and then fit the pieces together. If you've ever done a puzzle, you might recall the anxiety you felt until some pieces (usually the border) began to fit together, the adrenaline rush that overtook you as more and more of the pieces meshed and the picture emerged, and the feeling of gratification that settled over you as the last puzzle piece found its home.

Phase III of an I-Search unit is more challenging for several reasons. First, you don't start out with a box of puzzle pieces. Rather, you have to search for the puzzle pieces yourself. In doing so, you're likely to mix in loose pieces from other puzzles, which can be very confusing. As you try to assemble your puzzle, you're

constantly deciding if a particular piece does or does not belong. Second, although you have your question as a guide, you don't begin with a gestalt. Simultaneously, you are creating a final picture as you are discovering what that picture looks like.

When doing a jigsaw puzzle, you might be lucky enough to have some helpers with extra pairs of eyes or advice. In an I-Search, students also have assistance from teachers who provide support; guide the way; and create safeguards so that students do, indeed, find the right puzzle pieces and meaningfully connect them.

Phase III might also be more rewarding than doing a jigsaw puzzle. Teachers report that toward the end of Phase III, when the shape of the puzzle is becoming clearer and most of the pieces are joined, they see their students visibly relax. Students pause, feeling momentarily relieved that they are making meaning. Then, they marshal their energy for the final phase, where they will bring to closure the meaning-making process. Finally, they will revel in a real feeling of well-earned satisfaction.

Just as students feel ready to move on to Phase IV after the hard work of Phase III, so do we. The next chapter describes Phase IV, showing how students can convey what they have learned in relation to their question and what they have learned about themselves as researchers.

Representing Knowledge

In October 1347, a ship sailed from Caffa to Messina. The ship contained silks, rugs, and perfumes from exotic countries. It was a very special day for the town's people. They all gathered around to buy, sell, and trade. No one noticed that large rats, which carried hundreds of fleas, were climbing off the ship and onto ropes into the town. The rats carried bubonic diseases. The people of the town noticed the large populations of rats but paid no attention. Soon, the rats got to the homes of the people in the town. The fleas bit the rats who then became carriers of the disease. The fleas started to multiply and lay eggs. The fleas bit the people who lived in the households, giving them the disease.

This excerpt comes from a paper written by a 7th grade student in Indianapolis. His I-Search question was, "What were the causes and effects of the Black Death [Bubonic Plague] in Russia in the 1300s?" If we had the opportunity to read the student's entire paper, see the posters he created for his exhibition, and listen to his presentation; we would see that he was able to do the following:

• *Convey* with rigor what he had learned in relation to his search question.

• *Explain* the inquiry process he had carried out to build his knowledge over a period of time.

• *Think* critically about the content by expressing, for example, a critique, an evaluation, a comment, or a recommendation (e.g., "One out of every four people in a town survived the plague. It's very hard to believe that a plague could wipe out that much love, loyalty, and friendship. . . . If you were the only survivor, it must have been very lonely knowing that all of your family was dead").

• *Reflect on* the skills and abilities he developed as a researcher and can apply in the future (e.g., "I have learned how to develop a hypothesis . . . how to set priorities so I do things when they have to be done").

These four aspects of content and process knowledge naturally flow one into the other. The mobius strip, a continuous, double-looping ribbon, is the perfect image for conveying these goals of inquiry (see Figure 5.1). In this chapter, we explore how teachers encourage students to represent their knowledge through I-Search papers and exhibitions.

Teachers Align Process and Product

For Macrorie (1988), the father of the I-Search concept, a written essay, or paper, is the natural outgrowth of the inquiry process: "A person conducts a search to find out something he needs to know for his own life and writes the story of his adventure" (Preface, n.p.). Macrorie's basic premise is that writing allows students to organize their ideas and convey meaning to others. Caine and Caine (1991) concur: "We acquire deeper insights in part as we find clearer ways to talk about and describe what we are learning and what it means to us" (p. 122). The English Language Arts Standards (National Council of Teachers of English and the International Reading Association, 1996) hold teachers accountable for helping students learn how to write a report to effectively communicate in writing. An I-Search paper is an excellent vehicle for teaching writing and fostering writing development for all

students, even those who are resistant, hesitant, or disabled writers.

If a traditional research paper is like a trip to the dentist, then the I-Search paper is more like an outing to a park. It has a nonintimidating, user-friendly format with the following sections (see Appendixes A-2, A-3, and A-4 for these criteria and other guidelines):

• My Search Question (What was my question? Why did I care about this? What did I already know as I started my search?)

• My Search Plan (What is the story of my search? What materials and resources did I use? What helped or hindered my work? How did I overcome problems?)

• What Information Did I Learn as a Result of My Search (What are the important ideas? How do these ideas link to one another in a meaningful way? What information or evidence supports these ideas?)

• What This Content Means to Me (What conclusions can I draw? What interpretations can I make? What next questions interest me?)

• What I Have Learned About Myself as a Researcher (What can I now do that will help me be a researcher in the future? What are my next goals?)

• References

• Appendixes

Young adolescents are drawn to the I-Search paper for four reasons. First, they like being able to visibly insert themselves in the paper through the liberal use of the pronoun *I*. With permission to personalize, they are more willing to reveal their own insights and feelings in relation to what they are learning.

FIGURE 5.1
Mobius Strip

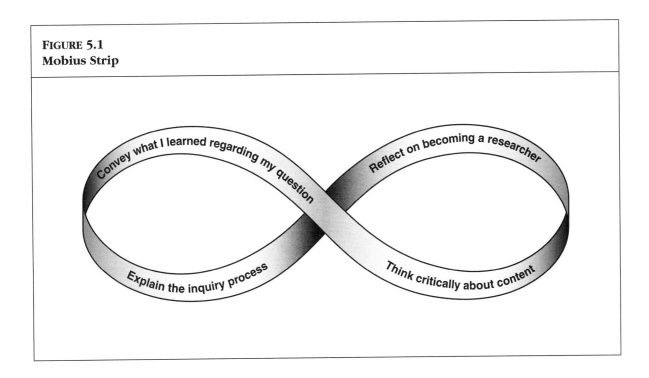

Second, it gives them authentic practice with a commonly accepted outline used by the research community (e.g., research questions/ hypotheses, research methodology, findings, conclusions, future steps). As students carry out investigations in high school, postsecondary schools, in the workplace, or graduate school, they are likely to encounter this basic outline, with slight variations. Thus, they will have built a foundation in middle school for this later work.

Third, the format relates process to product. In the I-Search Unit, students pose a question in Phase I, develop a search plan in Phase II, and gather and integrate information in Phase III. Students can draft sections of the outline as an ongoing part of the inquiry process.

Fourth, the format becomes a welcoming context for using varied media, allowing students to display their multiple talents, creative abilities,

and multiple intelligences. For example, one student discovered the poem "Whales Weep Not" by D. H. Lawrence in the *Norton Anthology of Modern Poetry* (Ellman & O'Clair, 1988) during her search. She felt particularly drawn to this stanza:

> And enormous mother whales lie dreaming suckling their whale-tender young and dreaming with strange whale eyes wide open in the waters of the beginning and the end (p. 369).

Later, in writing a lead for her paper, she found a creative outlet to personalize her writing. She incorporated language from the poem that was particularly evocative:

> There is so much more to a whale's life than just a quiet afternoon in the sea. If only we could see through the whale's gentle eyes to the feelings of their unhappy past. Whales have been through

a lot considering their species has been close to extinction and threatened for a while. I have previously studied whales, but only the good side of their lives. . . .

In addition to papers, and sometimes in lieu of a written report, students demonstrate their knowledge using a variety of media and formats. Depending on their talents and abilities, students may choose virtually any medium:

- Create a multimedia presentation.
- Produce a videotape.
- Draw a mural.
- Design a Web site.
- Write and enact a short play.
- Create a newsletter.
- Hold a debate.
- Create a slide show.
- Sew a quilt.

The goal of exhibitions is for students to find a productive and generative way to convey their substantive understandings (McDonald, Barton, Smith, Turner, & Finney, 1993).

In Phase IV of an I-Search Unit, teachers assist students with representing knowledge in a paper, in an exhibition, or both. To reach this point, teachers have done both *forward* and *backward* planning (McDonald, 1992). Planning forward, teachers set expectations at the very beginning of the unit and explained how the four phases build on each other. They have made explicit the connection between process and product. Planning backward, teachers have been clear about desired outcomes and have made sure that students have the support they need for carrying out the process. They have been carefully assessing student work all along by asking questions like these:

- Does each student have a solid question?
- Does each search plan work?
- Are students gathering information using varied resources?
- Are they making meaning?

If teachers are dissatisfied with their answers, they immediately provide students with the assistance they need. By the time students enter Phase IV, they have a portfolio that contains plans, notes, drafts, and a journal with their reflections.

As the remaining sections of this chapter show, teachers take responsibility for setting the specific criteria for papers and exhibitions and reviewing these criteria with students; engaging students in the process of drafting, reviewing, redrafting, and editing; and organizing a celebratory event.

Teachers Set and Review Criteria

Teachers set criteria to make explicit what they expect from students in terms of content and process. Teachers derive these expectations from three sources:

- An understanding of developmental abilities of young adolescents.
- A recognition of what national, state, or local standards are calling for.
- A respect for what families and the community desire as student outcomes.

The criteria provide a focus for teacher assessment, peer review of the work in progress, and student self-assessment. Herman, Aschbacher, and Winters (1992) explain that carefully crafted criteria help students evaluate their own work in progress, as well as their completed work (see Appendixes A-2 through A-7 for specific criteria that students and teachers can use for ongoing assessment).

In Phase I, when students pose their I-Search question, they state what they already know. This serves as an initial marker for the student, as well as teachers and peers, to measure the distance students have come by the time they conclude Phase IV. What they are doing is defining the *zone of proximal development,* the distance between current levels of knowledge and levels that can be accomplished by having undertaken a search for knowledge (Vygotsky, 1978). This measuring of distance allows students to prove to themselves that they can succeed in taking responsibility for learning and handle the risks that accompany this endeavor. As one student noted:

> Making my own decisions and taking risks was scary at first, but it all came together at the end. I am proud of myself and I think it all paid off. I faced my problems and enjoyed my topic. I thought this project was going to lead me to some turbulence, but I landed safely. I . . . enjoyed the flight.

Scoring criteria and rubrics make public to students, parents, and others the basis for judging student work. For example, for the section "My Search Question," teachers might decide on the following criteria:

• Have a strong lead or good opening. Draw the reader into the topic with a good lead—for example, a story, quote, questions, or startling statement.

• State your research question as clearly as possible. Show how it relates to the theme and overarching concepts of the unit.

• Explain your personal interest or connection with the question. Why did you care about the question?

• Tell what you already knew about the topic when you began the search.

Appendixes A-5 and A-6 present a scoring guide (with criteria and rubrics compiled from several different classrooms) for the entire I-Search paper. This guide easily integrates other media. Although this example does not address mechanics, style, or a knowledge of specific rhetorical conventions, teachers usually include these components.

Whether students are preparing an I-Search paper in written form, a multimedia presentation, or an exhibition, teachers place a high value on content and process. The next section describes in detail what teachers value, first with respect to content and then with respect to process.

Content Criteria

In terms of content, teachers want students to be able to display a fluency with and sense of ownership of the content; provide evidence that they have thought critically about the content; and generate a new set of questions to be explored in the future.

Student's Work Displays a Fluency with Content. Building on the meaning making that is the hallmark of Phase III, teachers want to see that students have internalized information and can converse fluently about it in their own words. Teachers help students to meaningfully organize their content within their report or exhibition so that there is an internal logic related to the content. The Standards for the English Language Arts (National Council of Teachers of English, 1996) value students' being able to generate a text structure that is driven by content. A good organizational structure reveals that the student has made meaningful interconnections among ideas.

For example, Andrew, a student in Bedford, was pursuing a question that focused on the effect the whaling industry had on New England's economy. Propelled by the content he had found, he chose to organize his information under two major headings: the profit and the loss. Other students used other text structures. Pateen, in Lawrence, who focused on photography, used thesis, argument, and conclusion. Lizzie, also from Lawrence, who was studying genetic disorders, listed specific examples in a series. Derek, in Bedford, used a cause-and-effect structure to convey information about government regulations and the declining fish population. Jose, in California, relied on a chronology to present information about the key battles in World War I.

For many students, a narrative structure is the best vehicle for representing content knowledge. The reason might be, as Caine and Caine (1991) suggest, that the organization of information in story form is a natural brain process. They also note that stories are powerful because they "bind" information and understanding. Macrorie (1988, Preface, n.p.) says, "I-Search Papers tell stories of quests that counted for the questors and they are written in a way that catches and holds readers." For example, a student from

Bedford used a narrative to reveal his fluency with content:

Soon, other whaling towns began to make huge whaling ships to keep up with Nantucket's booming industry. Bigger boats were needed because the whales were depleted close to the island. The whalers had to stock more supplies to whale for a longer period of time at greater distances from home. Nantucket was starting to become the whaling capital instead of New Bedford. However, this would soon backfire on Nantucket's whaling industry forever!!

In the small harbor of Nantucket, there happened to be a rather large sandbar. This sandbar was just small enough for the whalers not to notice it when they had smaller boats. This sandbar was very noticeable with the huge whaling boats that the Nantucket fishermen were making. The boats could just barely make it over the sandbar with no cargo in them; but with any cargo whatsoever, they couldn't go over it without hitting the top of the bar. So the only way to solve this problem was to have the whaling boats anchor out beyond the sandbar. The barges would travel out to get the barrels of oil from the ships, take them back to the dock, and then take them to the candle factories. This process took many extra hours to complete, and soon New Bedford surpassed Nantucket and the whaling industry began to die away in Nantucket. The decrease in the whaling industry meant the loss of jobs and many people left the island to try and find jobs elsewhere. Soon, Nantucket's whaling industry died out all together, and just about every industry departed, except for the small stores and shops.

Content presented as a narrative is not necessarily superficial or lacking in depth. In fact, the content knowledge contained in this excerpt relates to middle school standards in social studies (National Council for the Social Studies, 1994). The student was able to "use economic concepts to help explain historical and current development and issues in local, national, or global contexts" (p. 43) and "describe the role that supply and demand, price, incentives, and profits play in determining what is produced and distributed in a competitive market system" (p. 41). The presentation style, however, shows a comfortable fluency with these big, important ideas.

Along with strong content, teachers want to see evidence of critical thinking.

Student's Work Contains Evidence of Critical Thinking. Presseisen's 1985 definition of critical thinking, based on the work of Jozef Cohen (1971) is one with which many teachers can resonate:

> Using basic thinking processes to analyze arguments and generate insight into particular meanings and interpretations; develop cohesive, logical reasoning patterns and understand assumptions and biases underlying particular positions (Presseisen, p. 45).

Thinking critically about content has been a prominent feature of immersion in Phase I and meaning making in Phase III. In Phase IV, teachers want students to demonstrate in their reports and exhibitions that they can offer opinions, make judgments, evaluate, critique, form conclusions, make predictions, and offer recommendations for themselves and others. As in Phase III, teachers can foster critical thinking by giving students opportunities for discussion, valuing reflection, helping students use graphic organizers to see relationships, and using varied tools for analysis. Drawn from several classrooms, Figure 5.2 (see next page) lists representative examples of students' critical thinking.

One kind of critical thinking, making a recommendation, is a compelling way for young adolescents to address problems relating to the real world. It gives them practice in moving from the personal to the global (Beane, 1990; Jacobs, 1989). It adds to their prestige as thinkers. Students begin to understand that there are larger, more fundamental issues in the world and that their search connects to these. It also helps them realize that there can be solutions to problems, and that solutions come from people like them. The following two examples are from students in Lawrence and Bedford:

> Charity is another way to help the homeless. . . . Charity isn't only donating a large amount of money or objects. Even if you only donate a penny a day, or put a quarter into a charity box in a store, that money is still going to someone who really needs it. Just think about it. If you donated penny a day for a year, it would make $3.65. If each person did that, it would be a lot of money going to a good cause. Just imagine. Some families have no money and no food and are just wandering around the streets. If you donated even just a little bit of money, you can put a hot meal in front of that family's face. If you are in a store and you see a charity box on the checkout counter, drop a quarter into it. It can make a difference. Remember, every little bit helps.

FIGURE 5.2
Examples of Critical Thinking from Student Work

Type of Critical Thinking	Example from Student Work
Changing a belief	(Animal experimentation) What I have learned during the course of I-Search is enough to drastically change my life. It's like every time I wash my hands or my hair, I'll start thinking about what died for it. It's enough to make me buy cruelty-free products. Also, I feel better about myself when I only use cruelty-free products because it just makes me feel like a more humane person. Besides that, I will probably feel differently towards companies that use animal testing. (Rachel, New York)
Making a judgment	Job training programs have also been cut over the past 10 years. It would be easier and cheaper to train people to work than to support them on welfare for the rest of their lives. (Karen, New York)
Seeing different viewpoints	Some people are proud of New England as a leading whaling port. Others are ashamed that we slaughter so many creatures just to bring products to our homes. Regardless of which side of the issue they are on, everyone shares a belief that it is an important part of history to learn about. (Anna, Bedford)
Offering an opinion	My opinion is that the [Pine Barrens] fire is over, there is nothing else you can do about the fire except learn about it for the next time there is a fire. (Stacy, New York)
Making a prediction	. . . the lobster source will dwindle and probably be depleted in the near future. Unless lobstermen slow down the rate at which they are catching lobsters, or they change the method of lobstering considerably, the lobster industry doesn't have a very good chance of surviving. (Nathan, Bedford)
Forming a conclusion	We have learned that we need to conserve our rivers because we can't get new water, we have to keep using the same water over and over. We also know that it takes a lot to clean water and we don't always have that money, so we need to take care of what we have while we have it. Not only did we learn that, but we learned that it takes a lot more water to do some of the things that we do in our daily habits than we might have thought when we first started this project. (group of students, Indianapolis)

FIGURE 5.2—*(continued)* **Examples of Critical Thinking from Student Work**	
Type of Critical Thinking	**Example from Student Work**
Appreciating	We think, from now on, we will never take clean water for granted. After this, we are grateful for our clean parks and semi-clean rivers. We are glad that we live in the United States and have ready access to clean water and health care. We will try harder to conserve water. We understand that without rivers, many great civilizations would never have existed. (Shawna, Indiana)
Seeing implications	I know now to listen to the directions in a blizzard, or any disaster. Because if I don't, I might get seriously hurt or maybe even get killed. (Tyronne, Indiana)

Polluting [wetlands] like this must stop. Reusing and recycling must be stressed, and we have to pick up any trash that we see on the ground anywhere. Other ways of helping are writing to the government about new laws to protect wetlands or joining protection groups. Perhaps, though, the most important thing of all is to learn more about the problem and to educate everyone you can. If more people know how big a problem it is, with a little hard work it can be solved.

Thinking critically often prompts students to generate more questions and to keep the inquiry process alive.

Student's Work Generates Next Questions. Questions beget questions. The defining characteristic of lifelong learning is to be able to identify questions to explore. Teachers want students to generate a new set of questions within their report or exhibition to show that this inquiry does not end with this product. In the

following examples, students' questions build on what they have learned:

I would like to research cod fishing and compare it to whaling because now I know so much about the collapse of whaling that I hope I would be able to compare it to the overharvesting of cod.

Now I am particularly interested in the long-term effects that environmental tobacco smoke has on adults from childhood exposure.

The things I would like to explore further are the animals in the Pine Barrens, the types of food they eat, the types of plants that grow there, and many other things. The main area in the future I would want to focus on is the ecosystem of the Pine Barrens.

Armed with growing research skills, students feel confident that they can continue to be investigators. This is the second kind of knowledge teachers want students to represent. Teachers want students to be able to tell the story of their search and also look inward to appreciate their own development as researchers.

Process Criteria

The following are kinds of evidence that show how much students have learned about the process of conducting research.

Students Tell the Story of the Search. The first goal teachers set is for students to be able to provide a chronicle of their search process. The following excerpt by Ariel, a student in Lawrence, is a personal account of what she did as she carried out her search on special effects in the movies:

> When I first set out to research, . . . I decided to use the UMI system on the school library's computer to find citations for magazines which had articles on special effects. I had never used this system before, but I soon found out it was quite simple to use. I got a list of seven or so citations in the time period I had on the computer. Walking back to my seat to look at my list, I got distracted by a book I saw on the shelf. It proved to have excellent information on everything I needed and I would later find out it would be my best source of information.
>
> Next, I went to the index to the SIRS books. I found an article that suited my topic, and set out to find the book. I found my book after having some trouble locating it and read the article which had minimal information. But I did get a good quote. I finally used my computer list and found two articles in magazines which also had little information, but did give me some insight into the movie industry's plans of using special effects in the future.

> I had some difficulties finding the right magazines and I didn't get as much information as I would have liked. . . . It was extremely frustrating (I don't think I'll laugh about it until I'm out of college) sorting through all the stacks of magazine and never finding that one little issue of *Rolling Stone* that could have really helped my project. Encyclopedias weren't much help. . . . I also interviewed Vivian Guarino who works on special effects in New York City.

This excerpt shows Ariel's ability to evaluate resources, apply specific library skills within an authentic context, and realize that careful research can be enhanced by good luck. It is through self-assessment and reflection that students appreciate their own development as researchers.

Students Show Appreciation of Their Own Development as Researchers. The second goal is for students to engage in self-assessment and reflection about the acquisition of research skills. At the beginning of the unit, teachers want students to set goals based on areas of need. For example, one student talked about his problem of talking on the phone; he wasn't clear about what information he was seeking. But by doing an I-Search, he found that he "learned what question to ask to get the answers I wanted."

Teachers delight in hearing students say, "I have found new ways to get information and make meaning." For example, one student in Long Beach, California, changed his perception of museums. Before the I-Search, he viewed them as only as places with "weird pictures." But after visiting the Museum of Tolerance in Los

Angeles (devoted to the Holocaust), he realized that "there are many different kinds of museums and you can get good information there." Figure 5.3 (see next page) presents specific examples of the kinds of skills students say they have developed: interview skills, developing strategies, taking responsibility to meet a deadline, making decisions as independent learners, becoming a helper to someone else.

Last, teachers want students to set new goals to expand their research skills. For example, one student noted, "I am not as creative as I want to be when it comes to writing. I hope I can achieve my goal by the end of the school year." This kind of reflection allows students to look within, appreciate growth, and see that learning is a lifelong process.

Teachers Create Cycles of Drafting and Reviewing

Student drafting in Phase IV is a continuation of the writing and analysis that they began in Phase I. For example, in Phase I, teachers encouraged students to begin writing about their question. Because students kept journals of the search process, they continuously wrote about the ups and downs of implementing the search plan they had developed in Phase II. Each use of an analysis tool in Phase III (e.g., cause and effect, pro and con, similarities and differences, and sequencing) became the basis for drafting paragraphs about findings and interpretations. If teachers have had students create drafts on a word processor, then previous draft sections can be combined to produce a full first draft. Some

teachers find a real benefit in using the *Search Organizer* software because all previous work is automatically saved in the relevant place within a report outline. Thus, students begin Phase IV with a solid working draft.

Once a first draft exists, teachers can guide students to revise their work. By providing students with a rubric, teachers can show students how each successive draft can more closely approximate the desired standard. For example, Figure 5.4 (on p. 88) shows a rubric for the first section of the I-Search Paper: My Search Question (see Appendix A-6 for other rubrics).

To help students learn how to develop a captivating lead that arouses an audience's attention, the teachers in Lawrence designed a minilesson for Phase IV. First, teachers and students discussed common conventions for arousing interest (e.g., asking a question, presenting a startling fact, or offering a quote). Then, teachers provided examples drawn from magazines and newspaper articles. Students benefited from seeing the techniques, strategies, and approaches that others use in the creative process (Sternberg & Williams, 1996). Next, small cooperative groups brainstormed different leads for a sample report. Later, each student had a chance to draft leads for his or her own paper and confer with a fellow student to obtain feedback. What follows are two sample products of this carefully planned minilesson:

> [Topic: sexual abuse] You can't run, and you can't hide, but you can get help. This is the truth, but to girls that this happened to, they think differently.
> [Topic: the Pine Barrens] Fearful firefighters filled the streets as the fire

FIGURE 5.3
Examples of Specific Research Skills Students Say They Have Developed

Specific Skill	Examples
Sharpened interviewing skills	The most important thing to me was probably learning how to do an interview. It will help me in life because it's a first hand resource, unlike a book or article that can be outdated. An interview gives you the most modern information and it's from someone who was there. (He had interviewed his cousin who had worked on Photo CDs at Kodak.)
Having an effective strategy	As a researcher, I found that starting out in small areas of my topic would help me with the big things. What I mean is that if I started out finding information right away from an encyclopedia or a book, I would be lost, I wouldn't know where to look. But if I started out small with microfiche and magazines, I would get ideas and it would be easier to work with larger forms of reference.
Taking responsibility to meet a deadline	I will forever respect researchers. The most important thing I learned is how to meet a deadline. I also learned a lot of responsibility. I mean, not like I didn't have any before I started this project, but I gained more throughout this project.
Making decisions as an independent learner	I also made some independent decisions about my writing. When I came to a problem in my writing, I did not automatically ask the teacher for help. I first tried my best to work it out on my own.
Becoming a helper	I helped other people by helping them think of ideas of what kind of questions they should ask for their interview and when I found something related to their topic, I let them know.

spread 650 feet per hour. Covered in smoke and soot, they continued to control the blaze. Firefighters watched in fear as a propane tank traveled down the highway. Worries of its blowing up filled everyone with cries. People evacuated as soon as possible. The sky was no longer blue; the color kept changing from orange to black. This all began around 2 p.m. on Thursday afternoon, August 31,

1995. This was the news I heard two days after I came home from camp. I was so upset, because I had a lifetime of memories there. As a child, I went out to the Westhamptons every weekend to visit my grandparents. Once a month, we would take a hike on a nature preserve trail. The days we spent together will never be forgotten, because my grandpa died when I was only four.

Other minilessons may focus on how to make an oral presentation that rivets an audience, how to seamlessly integrate graphics with text, or how to structure the flow of a video. Teachers also help students revise and edit their work so that reports and exhibitions will display the following characteristics:

- *Completeness*. Each part of the overall report or exhibition is complete. It does not contain irrelevant information,

- *Creativity*. Students demonstrate imagination and originality. They use available resources and tools to creatively convey information.

- *Style*. The author's style is appropriate to the medium and to the purpose of the writing. The work reflects its author's distinctive use of language.

- *Media*. A variety of media are appropriately incorporated in a coherent and meaningful way.

- *Affect*. The author conveys passion, enthusiasm, pride of accomplishment, and a desire to help others learn.

- *Convention and mechanics*. Students use correct usage, whatever the medium.

Teachers review what they mean by each of these characteristics, provide students with models, review drafts, and give students suggestions for strengthening their work.

Teachers Organize Celebratory Events

A celebratory event is a time set aside for students to display or exhibit their work to an audience. Teachers, with input from students, plan the logistics: Who will be invited? When should it be held? How will it be organized? What will be shown, demonstrated, or exhibited? Sometimes, each individual student shows his or her work; at other times, groups of students make presentations. Just as each student can represent knowledge in many ways, teachers and students can design these activities in different ways. Here are some examples:

- In Indianapolis, at the end of a unit on water pollution and conservation, the teachers and students planned an after-school event. In addition to the 125 students, more than 200 parents and friends attended. Each student was assigned to a large table in the cafeteria, which displayed his or her I-Search paper, poster, diorama, or experiment. Nearby, a VCR was playing pretaped student skits and short plays. The visitors circulated from table to table, admiring the students' work, listening attentively to explanations, asking clarifying questions, and making links across different projects.

- In Pennsylvania, students organized a health fair modeled after the health fair that began the unit as a kickoff immersion activity in Phase I. The presenters at the original health fair had been health professionals; this time, the presenters were students who assumed roles of professionals in health-related fields.

- In Milford, New Hampshire, students produced written papers enhanced with graphics and charts. At the end of the unit, students brought their finished papers to a final event. Sitting in a circle, each student took a turn sharing the most important ideas and reading his or her favorite paragraph. The papers were then placed in the school library where other students in later

FIGURE 5.4
Rubric for Evaluating I-Search Paper: Section: My Search Question

Criterion	4	3	2	1
Strong Lead	Arouses reader interest; draws reader into the topic using a captivating lead	Awareness of audience; uses some enticing ways to engage audience	Provides matter-of-fact introduction; little awareness of audience	No lead
Question Stated	Question is clearly stated and makes strong link to overarching concepts as appropriate	Question is clearly stated; mention is made of overarching concepts, but link is tenuous	Question is poorly stated; weak link to overarching concepts	No question and /or no connection to overarching concepts
Personal Connection	Detailed explanation of why question is motivating	Some explanation of why question is motivating	Unclear explanation of personal connection	No explanation of personal connection
Starting Point	Detailed description of starting point	Some information provided	Unclear or sketchy information provided	No description of starting point

Scoring Note: A score of 4 is excellent; 3, good; 2, fair; 1, poor. See Appendix A-6 for suggested rubrics for all sections of the I-Search paper.

years could borrow them.

• In Bedford, students formed groups based on both teacher and student input. Each group created a TV-like quiz show (e.g., Jeopardy) that allowed students to use information from their searches on the Atlantic Ocean. As each group performed for the others, the teacher videotaped their work. This allowed the performers themselves, as well as others, to watch the video as often as they pleased. Repeated viewings helped

students with self-evaluation and allowed them to generate additional ideas. In addition, students hung artwork and poetry and other works on the school walls. For example, this poem, "The Atlantic Ocean: The River of Dreams," was prominently displayed:

When I look outside,
and see the gulls screeching
over that endless sea of Indigo.
I wonder what the world would be like

without fish and sea anemone
even without the great white shark.
The ocean is everything,
everything that lives and breathes,
everything that laughs and cries and loves.
She who searches for the shells under the
    rocks,
and discovers a small crab instead,
squeals with delight as it climbs up her
    shoulder.
I know I will always *wonder*
what the world would be like without the
    ocean,
But I know, I will never ask.

When the audience includes other students, teachers, families, and friends, the student is perceived and honored as a contributing member of the learning community. Every student doing an I-Search has become a resident expert, having "majored" in a topic within the framework of the unit's theme and concepts (Brown & Campione, 1996). Each student has something valuable to contribute to the overall knowledge base of classmates and others. One student said that just as he had interviewed experts to carry out his search, people could interview him, because he was an expert. Some students want what they have learned to improve the lives of others. For example, one student in Lawrence was motivated to disseminate information:

> I'm glad that I found a lot of information. . . . I'm hoping that many people will read this and learn enough from it so that they can help someone that they know with an eating disorder or so that they will not form one themselves. It's a horrible thing, and I hope that this report will help as many people as possible.

Whereas the culminating or celebratory event gives students recognition as learners, it also places them in somewhat of a risky situation. Students are holding up the meaning they have made to scrutiny, allowing others to judge the validity of what they have found (Macrorie, 1988). Members of the audience assess whether information is accurate, complete, and worthwhile. If, however, they do identify gaps or misconceptions, they might offer additional information or suggestions for further exploration. This dynamic interaction between students and their audience offers students an opportunity to learn about giving and receiving feedback.

Many teachers hand out diplomalike certificates. In fact, teachers in Indianapolis made the certificate-awarding ceremony almost like a graduation. In front of the large assembly of parents and friends who attended the celebration, teachers acknowledged each student's individual accomplishment (e.g., "Johnny designed an excellent survey that allowed him to gather information about disasters" and "Yvonne learned how to use graphing software to display her findings").

Students, too, have often taken it on themselves, in a planned or spontaneous way, to congratulate their teachers. One student in Milford, New Hampshire, stood up after all the reports were read and "extemporaneously thanked the teachers for their hard work and help on behalf of the class and said how great the unit had been" (Zorfass et al., 1991, p. 11.86). It was clear to see that the burst of applause from the remaining students was genuine.

Final Comments

The report or exhibition traditionally marks the end of the I-Search Unit. But the goal of the I-Search is to promote active researching—not just for an eight-week span of time during early adolescence, but for a lifetime. Recently, I sat lodged between an elderly couple, married for more than 50 years, on a flight from Chicago to Des Moines. Eager to talk, they told me that they were homeward bound after having just spent the last 21 days on safari in Nairobi. I realized that their travelogue followed a familiar pattern. They told me what they had hoped to learn, why they had gone, what they knew beforehand, what they learned, and what they thought about the experience. Here was a couple of unschooled I-Searchers par excellence. Watching and listening to them, I recognized another striking similarity between this couple relating tales of their safari and the young adolescents I had seen describing their search stories. I saw the same glint in their eyes that comes with acquiring knowledge through active research.

The last chapter of this book focuses on the Make It Happen! approach. It describes what is necessary at the school and district level to design, implement, and hone an I-Search Unit over time.

Implementing Active Research

I get the distinct impression from the examples used in this book that the I-Search Unit is for interdisciplinary teams. What about individual teachers? Can't they do an I-Search Unit too?

It can't be spontaneous combustion that ignites the I-Search Unit? Who lights the spark?

It didn't take too much reading between the lines to realize that an I-Search Unit requires careful curriculum design. What does the design process involve?

Is there any one factor that accounts for successful implementation of the unit?

What prevents this unit from being a one-round innovation? Do teachers evaluate what they have done to learn from their experience and strengthen the unit in the future?

What kind of facilitation, by internal or external facilitators, is needed, especially if teams are involved?

Curriculum reform always requires the support of central office or middle school administrators. What's the organizational support for the I-Search?

We're guessing that questions similar to these may have crossed your mind as you read the previous chapters. Our presumption is borne of experience. Teachers, curriculum coordinators, principals, and assistant superintendents have often approached us with insightful questions like these. Because we delight in these kinds of queries—that strike at the heart of successful implementation—we've chosen to use them as the organizing frame for this chapter. Our goal is to highlight key factors that affect the successful implementation of I-Search Units.

Involving Interdisciplinary Teams or Individual Teachers

No one owns the I-Search; there are no rules about who can do an I-Search. Ken Macrorie's book, *The I-Search Paper* (1988), started the active-research ball rolling. We surmise that many teachers (especially English language arts and social studies teachers) got hooked on the idea after reading Macrorie's book or attending a conference. Drawing on available books and articles (Joyce & Tallman, 1997; Kaszyca & Krueger, 1994) and EDC's Make It Happen! materials (1991, 1996; including the *Search Organizer* software, 1996), they probably created versions of the I-Search that worked for them. Grassroots efforts probably encouraged the spread of the idea as early innovators shared strategies and instructional materials with others. We base this conclusion on the number of presentations by teachers we see listed on agendas for educational conferences, as well as the e-mail inquiries, telephone calls, and correspondence we receive.

Macrorie's 1988 book also motivated us to mold the I-Search into a curriculum unit that could be carried out by interdisciplinary teams. We saw the potential to wed strong, developmentally appropriate curriculum with one of the hallmarks of middle school reform—interdisciplinary education. Over the past decades, as the middle school reform movement has gained momentum, more and more middle schools are organizing themselves into interdisciplinary teams. When George and Shewey conducted a survey in 1994, they found that 85 percent of the schools they contacted were organized into interdisciplinary teams. The number has probably grown since

then. A team in a middle school usually includes teachers from the core content areas (English language arts, mathematics, social studies, science, and sometimes foreign language and bilingual teachers).

Once schools establish interdisciplinary teams, teachers and administrators often want to make the most of this structure to benefit students. They search for worthwhile curriculums that can bind the teams together to meet the developmental needs of young adolescents. To us, the I-Search Unit seemed to be one compelling option. We also saw this unit as a way to expand the core team to include librarians, media specialists, computer teachers, and resource room or special education teachers.

Thus, our experience has been working with teams, although the composition of our teams might vary. We might work with the subset of a full team (just two or three teachers), or we might work with a full team of eight or nine teachers by including specialists. Over the years, we have found tremendous power and energy in working with teams. Some of the most obvious advantages are as follows:

- Teachers have the advantage of hearing multiple perspectives and drawing on them.
- Teachers share knowledge across disciplines in ways that enrich the interdisciplinary experience.
- Professional development occurs naturally as teachers work together and learn from one another.
- Teachers across the team share responsibility for students.
- By including media specialists and librarians, teams find and use more varied resources to

enrich the unit.

- By including special education teachers, teams are more likely to include students with learning problems or disabilities, and these students are less likely to fall through the cracks.

Lighting the Spark: The Local Champion

From our experience, the emergence of I-Search teams in a school or district is no accident. Rather, a key individual has usually emerged to light the spark. This person might be a curriculum coordinator, principal, staff developer, a middle school team leader, a school- or district-level curriculum coordinator, or an assistant superintendent. We have gradually come to refer to this person as a "local champion." Once this person envisions how an interdisciplinary team can meet both the needs of students and the needs of a school or district around teacher collaboration, the individual becomes a champion of the cause.

The local champion advocates for the adoption of I-Search Units by explaining to key administrators how the curriculum resonates with the district's mission and reform agenda. This was the case in Lowell, Massachusetts. Francene Donahue, a district-level desegregation facilitator, had discovered our work with I-Search Units through her networking at the state level. She diligently gathered literature about inquiry-based learning, discussed the need for change at the classroom level with middle school administrators and practitioners, and explained to them how an I-Search Curriculum Unit could meet their newly formulated middle school agenda. She then introduced the concept of the I-Search to the two key

central office administrators: the superintendent and her supervisor, Peter Stamas, the Desegregation Initiative Project Director. Once these administrators became excited about the concept, they, in turn, were willing to explore possible funding sources for introducing the approach and compensating the staff for time spent on curriculum design (Zorfass & Donahue, 1997). Francene was a successful local champion because she knew who else needed to be involved, had the capacity to work in tandem with them, and was willing to devote sustained time and substantial energy to igniting the spark.

After local champions solicit the needed district- or school-level support, they turn to the next critical task—recruiting teams of teachers. They do so by using several strategies. For example, they might devote a faculty meeting to presenting an overview of the I-Search, arrange for teachers to visit a school where the I-Search is being implemented, show one of EDC's videos from the Make It Happen! facilitator's guide and have a question-and-answer session afterwards, organize a study group to read and discuss relevant articles, or hold an awareness session that involves engaging teachers in a simulation.

As a result, the local champion might light the spark that ignites one team—or many; for example:

- One team—as Larry Aronstein, principal of the middle school in Bedford, Massachusetts, did with his 6th grade team.
- All three 7th grade teams—as Harriet Copel did when she was the assistant principal of the middle school in Lawrence, New York.
- All of the 6th, 7th, and 8th grade teams in one middle school—as Joyce Payne, district-level

administrator, did in collaboration with the princi-pal of Buck Lodge Middle School in Prince Geor-ge's County, Maryland.

- Teams from all nine magnet middle schools—as Francene Donahue did in Lowell, Massachusetts.

Local champions have found it is best to recruit teams by early winter of a school year so that by the springtime, start-up activities can begin. During the spring, teams can generate potential themes, further investigate inquiry-based learning, build team relationships, gather materials, and do an assets inventory of technol-ogy. Teams can then design curriculum in the summer and plan for implementation in the fol-lowing school year.

Designing the Curriculum Unit

A tremendous amount of planning and decision making goes into the design of an I-Search Unit. For example, teachers have to determine their theme and identify overarching concepts; clearly identify the desired outcomes related to stan-dards; craft the immersion activities for Phase I; determine the criteria for what students will *read, watch, ask,* and *do* in Phase II; plan who will take students to the library or media center to gather information in Phase III; determine which strategies will be used in Phase III to help stu-dents analyze information; develop rubrics for I-Search papers and exhibitions in Phase IV; and plan culminating events. Appendix A-8, "Curricu-lum Development Process," summarizes the key steps in the curriculum design process (and see

other helpful documents in the appendix, such as suggested rubrics in Appendix A-6). As we have worked with teams through this intensive process, we have learned three valuable lessons: to take time, to relate curriculum to standards and outcomes, and to collaborate.

Take Time

First, it takes time to design an I-Search unit. Most teams we have worked with use their sum-mer break for curriculum design. We've found that it takes a minimum of five days to do a thoughtful job. On paper, the process looks lin-ear, short, and easily doable. But in reality, it is recursive; teachers circle back to an earlier design step as their thinking becomes more aligned around a clear set of goals and strategies. For example, even when teachers think they are clear about their theme and overarching concepts, they often revisit these and make revisions. It is worth spending the time to brainstorm ideas, evaluate ideas against a set of criteria, debate what works best, and reach consensus at each step of the way (see Appendix A-1 for suggested criteria for immersion activities). The following example captures the back-and-forth discussion that occurred when the Bedford team was planning its Phase I activities:

> The oversized desktop calendar was filled with yellow Post-its. Each Post-it named a different Phase I immersion activity. "O.K.," said Lynda to her team-mates seated around the table. "Now it's time to look over our immersion activi-ties and evaluate them against our crite-ria. Do they relate to the theme and concepts? Will they help students develop concepts? Are the activities

motivating? Will they provoke students to pose questions?" After looking over the activities, teachers began making recommendations for shifting around Post-Its, deleting some and adding others.

For example, Marsha commented, "Before reading the newspaper articles about the Boston Harbor Cleanup, let's first bring in the speaker from the MWRA (Massachusetts Water Resources Association)."

"Yes," answered Bradd, the science teacher. "Let's also have students answer some reflection questions or write in their journals. We need a Post-It to remind us to have students engage in processing information."

You would have to multiply this moment many times over to have a full sense of what the curriculum design process actually involves.

Relate Curriculum to Standards and Outcomes

The second lesson we have learned is that teachers must be clear about their desired outcomes for students and how these outcomes link to the district, state, or national standards (see Chapter 1 for a discussion of some content standards). When teams of teachers in Long Beach, California, met to design their separate curriculum units, they each brought with them their newly minted local standards. Teachers found that the standards guided their work, helping them to articulate what they wanted students to achieve as active learners. At the same time, by having a curriculum unit to work on, they also felt that the standards came alive. As one teacher said, "Until now, those standards were just words on paper. But now I see how they can be

translated into my daily classroom experience." Once teachers are clear about standards, they can design stronger units, identify what tangible products they will collect from students, and develop rubrics to judge levels of performance (Jacobs, 1997).

Collaborate

Third, we have learned about the power of the collaborative process to promote professional development. By the end of a weeklong curriculum design process, teachers leave with a comprehensive, day-by-day curriculum unit (see Appendix A-9 for a typical Table of Contents). This document represents a mighty collaborative achievement that would not exist if every teacher had not learned something valuable from his or her colleagues. No single individual possessed all the knowledge or power that was critical for the design of the unit. These comments show us what teachers learn from one another through collaboration:

> The hardest part was coming up with overarching concepts. I expected this would be a breeze, but it wasn't. We had to do some research and hard thinking ourselves to figure out the big ideas. At first, I was afraid to reveal what I didn't know to the others. Sometimes I had trouble articulating my ideas. But my colleagues were patient and respectful. It wasn't just my ideas that took shape. Little by little, we all learned something valuable from each other and finally developed concepts that we were all proud of.

> This I-Search Unit is the perfect venue for changing my role. I've wanted to become more of a "guide on the side"

for a long time but didn't know how to do it. Now, with everyone's input, I have a set of working strategies I can't wait to try out.

I've never been pushed before to think about the implications of how what I do in my science classroom can affect how kids construct knowledge in other classrooms. My colleagues helped me see the connections.

We have seen that as a result of learning from one another, negotiating uncharted waters, and solving problems that affect what happens daily in classrooms, teachers change their beliefs, develop content knowledge, expand their repertoire of instructional and assessment strategies, and develop a sense of efficacy that they can meet student needs. These are often the fundamental goals of professional development programs.

Implementing the I-Search Unit

Depending on the theme, the desired outcomes, the age/grade of the students, and other curriculum demands, units can last 4–12 weeks. Some teams like to implement their units at the beginning of the school year to help their students develop an inquiry mind-set; others like to wait until later in the year to give students a chance to develop prerequisite research skills; and still others like to culminate the school year with the unit.

Conduct Ongoing Assessment

Regardless of when the unit occurs or how long it lasts, the critical factor for successful implementation is for teachers to engage in a process of ongoing assessment aimed at strengthening the unit while it is in process. To do this, teachers routinely gather evidence about student learning by reviewing student portfolios, observing students in action, listening to their conversations, and even interviewing students individually. In Indianapolis, we found that just having teachers ask students the two-part question, "What phase of the I-Search are you in, and what are you supposed to be doing?" provided insights into students' understanding of the active research process. Based on what teachers learn about what students think they should be doing, and what they are actually doing, they revise plans as needed, provide students with specific help and support, and readjust goals.

A team cannot do this kind of assessing and revising unless they meet frequently to coordinate their plans, discuss emerging issues, and brainstorm solutions. We cannot underestimate how much courage it takes to reflect and revise plans that were previously hammered out with sweat (even by teachers in Alaska in the winter). But teachers recognize that without an action/reflection stance during implementation, a unit can fall apart. For example, one team in Long Beach was three weeks into Phase I (immersion) of a unit on social unrest. Students' emerging questions filled the bulletin board: "Will they ever find a cure for AIDS? Who were the Zoot Suits? Is school drop out a big problem?" Although it was still early and these questions had potential, the team was not seeing evidence of a direct link between these questions and the unit's theme of social unrest. After some soul searching, the teachers admitted that their own fuzziness in defining social unrest was creating fuzzy thinking among students. They decided on a midcourse correction. By circling back to the U.S. Bill of Rights, they could explain how social unrest resulted when individuals or groups felt that their rights had been impinged on in some way. Within this context, the question about AIDS might be massaged into the following: "What has motivated the outcry for research dollars for AIDS? How can the government's response facilitate or impede unrest?"

Find Common Planning Time

In many middle schools today, interdisciplinary teams have daily periods set aside for common planning time. This time is a critical ingredient in making a team effort work. While in the throes of implementation, Susan, the language arts teacher, and her teammates in Indianapolis productively used their common planning time to solve emerging problems. They began their troubleshooting immediately on the second day of their unit on rivers. Susan began the meeting by clearly stating the problem:

> Remember when we planned the unit, we never got around to deciding on the specifics about how to introduce the unit. Even though each teacher took responsibility for saying something to the students on Day 1, we were not sure of exactly what each one of us planned to say. Now we're here on Day 2 and students are hearing different messages. They are already confused about what is expected of them.

The team did not argue with Susan's diagnosis. They fully agreed that the students' discomfort grew out of not knowing the expectations.

To solve the problem, they decided to agree on a coherent message to give the students. They reviewed the goals for each phase, the intended activities, and the requirements. Susan took notes on the board. Although the teachers only had a brief time to meet (their prep period was 40 minutes long), they still accomplished a great deal because they had a process they could follow. They identified and agreed on the problem and then found a solution that resulted in a clear action plan (Howard, 1993).

Beyond Round One: Evaluating to Strengthen the Unit for the Future

When local champions launch the I-Search, they have a vision that exceeds one round of implementation. They are usually savvy enough to recognize that the first round serves as a pilot—a chance for teachers and students alike to learn what active research is all about. It is through successive rounds, however, that teachers strengthen and deepen their efforts. What makes each successive round stronger is that teachers engage in evaluation after the unit ends. The evaluation component rounds out the cycle of curriculum design, implementation, and evaluation.

Hold a Retreat

Many teams hold a "Retreat" (or an "Advance," as one team in New Hampshire called it) to give themselves sufficient time for evaluation. Over the years, we have joined teams who held their retreats over lunch or dinner at a restaurant; at someone's house after a potluck dinner; or, unable to get away, during a series of meetings at school. Notwithstanding the location, the goal is always the same—to encourage teachers to evaluate the I-Search Unit by addressing the following four questions:

- What factors facilitated or hindered implementation of the unit?
- What was the effect of the unit on the students, on each one of us as professionals, and on the team as a whole?
- In what ways could we improve, expand, or deepen the unit in the future?
- Based on our experience, what advice would we give other teams just starting out?

Thoughtfully answering these questions requires gathering and analyzing data and then articulating findings. These steps heed Schmoker's (1996) call for educators to engage in continuous improvement. He asserts that educators should analyze what they have done against their results (effect on students). Through this analysis, teachers can make adjustments that significantly increase student achievement. By examining student work, the evaluation moves from general perceptions and impressions to a focus on student outcomes. Many teams have used an approach such as the following:

- Each teacher on the team selects a small number of students to focus on (perhaps two students, with varying abilities who did well, and one or two students, with varying abilities, who did not do as well as expected).
- Each teacher collects student work already assessed against a set of criteria or rubric (e.g.,

work samples filed in the portfolio, the journal, the final report, and the final exhibition).

- The teacher reviews the work and asks questions such as: Where do I find evidence of student success or lack of success? What factors might have come into play to promote or hinder success? What would I do differently to help other students like this one?
- The teacher shares the work, her analysis, and her recommendations with teammates.

Document What You Have Learned

One cycle of curriculum design, implementation, and evaluation provides teachers with the chance to learn from their experience. Iterative cycles offer them a chance to deepen and expand curriculum by translating what they have learned about curriculum, instruction, and assessment into practice. This was the case in Bedford. Figure 6.1 is a flashback to their pilot year. The vignette describes their Year 1 experience and the recommendations they made to strengthen the unit for the next round (which is the round we have drawn on for examples in this book).

The evaluation process has often been the impetus for expanding the I-Search Unit in ways that link to other middle school initiatives, such as thematic instruction, inquiry-based learning, and cooperative learning (see Figure 6.2, on p. 100). As a result of evaluation, teachers identify new areas to work on that build on what they have already accomplished. The following are ways in which teams have expanded their efforts.

- In Lowell, Massachusetts, one team deepened the assessment component during their second round of implementation. One of the

---

FIGURE 6.1
Bedford's Year 1 Recommendations

That first year of the I-Search, the teachers unanimously lacked confidence in their students' ability to be active researchers who posed their own questions. "I just don't think our 6th graders will get it," Lynda said, as the others nodded in agreement during their curriculum design. Bradd concurred, "They aren't ready to generate good research questions related to the overarching concepts."

Their theme that first year—"How does the Atlantic Ocean Affect Life in Massachusetts?"—had four overarching concepts related to aspects of life in Massachusetts: economy, environment, art and recreation, and community.

With the best of intentions of providing security and structure for their students, the team developed the following strategies. First, the teachers themselves generated a set of questions related to each overarching concept. Second, they formed We-Search Groups, cooperative groups where 3–4 students would work together on a similar We-Search question. Third, they asked each We-Search Group to pick an overarching concept for their group investigation. Fourth, they required each student within the cooperative group to select one of the teacher-generated questions.

Most cooperative groups zoomed in on the overarching concept related to the environment. They had two good reasons for doing so: (1) Students were comfortable with the content because most of the immersion activities had focused on this topic and (2) students assumed that there would be "tons" of available information since they already used a variety of materials and resources for the immersion activities. The teachers, however, wanted the students to choose varied topics and they were also afraid that students would compete for resources. So, the teachers "nudged" groups to pick another set of questions from the list. Students reluctantly complied, choosing the "teacher encouraged" topics.

When they later reflected on the completed unit, teachers noted that as the unit progressed, student work could be characterized as plodding rather than inspired. Indeed, students lacked a sense of ownership of the topic, one of the very goals of an I-Search. As Lynda perceived:

> I think one of the problems is that the questions did not come from the kids and it
> wasn't part of their thinking. Maybe each kid with some help from the teacher has
> to formulate the questions. Then, I think they'll own it and it will truly follow their
> own curiosity.

When it came time to make recommendations for the future, the team easily generated the following list:

- Refine and focus the theme and overarching concepts.
- Be explicit at the beginning about the entire process and goal.
- Have better and stronger immersion activities that help students elicit prior knowledge, build knowledge, and become provoked to learn more.
- Have students pose their own questions!

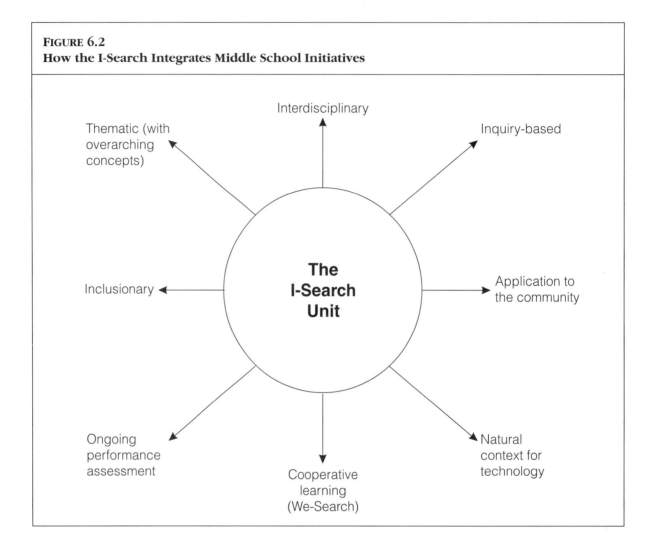

FIGURE 6.2
How the I-Search Integrates Middle School Initiatives

teachers who had been taking a graduate course in assessment did an independent study on developing rubrics. She used this knowledge to guide the team to develop rubrics for the I-Search Paper and exhibitions. This expansion meshed well with a priority within the district.

• At Buck Lodge Middle School in Maryland, the second round of implementation focused on clarifying expectations for exhibitions. This linked to the work the school was doing within the

ATLAS Project funded by the New American Schools (Orrell, 1996).

• The teachers in Indianapolis expanded their unit on disasters by linking the I-Search to community service. As Red Cross volunteers, students helped prepare readiness kits in the event a disaster struck.

• Many school districts in Indiana found that the I-Search was an excellent starting place for collaboration between regular and special education teachers. The active nature of the research, the use of varied materials and resources, and the ability to do an exhibition, all contributed to the successful participation of students with diverse disabilities. In each successive round of implementation, more students with disabilities were included in general education programs.

• Harriet Copel's middle school in Lawrence, New York, was fully committed to integrating technology into the curriculum. With Harriet's assistance, each year they found more ways to integrate CD-ROMs, computer simulations, graphing programs, spreadsheets, and word processing.

Facilitating the Process

I work with schools as an external facilitator to help them carry out cycles of designing, implementing, and evaluating I-Search Units. As an external facilitator who guides and models the process, my main goal has always been to build the leadership capacity of local facilitators who are internal to the district or school. One of my earliest experiences as an external facilitator was working with Harriet and her team in Lawrence. Through demonstration, modeling, and mentoring, I helped Harriet build her capacity as a local facilitator at her own school. Later, Harriet became an external facilitator at other schools. The training model Harriet and I forged in 1989 has served as the foundation for training local facilitators in other districts around the United States.

The local facilitator within a school or district might be a lead teacher, an assistant

superintendent or principal, a media specialist, or a curriculum coordinator. The recommended criteria for a facilitator are that the person:

• Has a firm grasp of inquiry-based learning in general and the I-Search process in particular.

• Understands the principles of adult development and can foster teacher growth.

• Has a flexible schedule that allows for convening meetings and gathering resources

• Is respected by the teachers, as well as the principal, for leadership abilities.

Using Harriet as the case in point, we can unpack the many roles the facilitator plays through the curriculum design, implementation, and evaluation cycle. Harriet has guided the curriculum design process in her school with three 7th grade teams. Her goal is to ensure that each unit has a good generative theme with strong overarching concepts; that activities promote inquiry and build in assessment; and that teachers use varied ways for students to convey what they have learned though written products and exhibitions.

Provide Support During Design

To make sure the teachers experience a sense of accomplishment, Harriet:

• Keeps people from feeling overwhelmed as they are asked to think simultaneously about desired goals, teaching activities, and ongoing assessment.

• Allows for one step to unfold after another (e.g., brainstorming activities, setting criteria for selecting activities, and applying criteria).

• Encourages the team to revisit an earlier step.

• Ensures that people document the plans they have agreed to implement.

• Knows when to introduce a new idea or relate ideas (e.g., when to bring up assessment).

• Paces the process so that there will be a sense of accomplishment after five days of design.

Like other effective facilitators, Harriet has learned when and how much to intervene during the curriculum design process. She seeks to achieve the right balance between knowing when to contribute ideas that can strengthen the design/content of the unit and when to withhold them. She and I have both found that if the facilitator allows her ideas to dominate the discussion, then teams may lose that critical sense of ownership. Facilitators need to recognize that teams want to implement their own ideas, not the facilitator's. At the same time, if the facilitator observes that the team is stuck, derailed, or has lost sight of the key concepts of the inquiry process, then it is appropriate to intervene to make sure that the unit embodies good teaching and creates a strong learning opportunity for students.

As a good facilitator, Harriet pays attention to interpersonal relationships, closely watching the dynamic interactions among teammates. A facilitator is often a negotiator, a "family therapist," and a mediator when personal and professional issues arise. Therefore, facilitators need to be good listeners, questioners, and diagnosticians to recognize what is and is not working. Once they identify what factors might be in operation, they can determine possible strategies to help a team work through any tension-causing issues. Figure 6.3 presents a brief vignette showing how one facilitator from Indiana, Mary-Pat Hatcher-Disler,

delicately resolved a conflict that could have halted the entire curriculum design process (M-P. Hatcher-Disler, "Notes on Facilitation," personal communication, 1994).

Encourage During Implementation

During implementation of the unit, Harriet, in her role as facilitator, made sure the team met regularly to:

• Review and refine past plans before implementation so everyone was "on the same page."

• Firm up logistics (e.g., which periods students will watch a particular movie).

• Check on follow-through (e.g., arranging for a field trip or speaker).

• Discuss student performance: Who is succeeding? Who is having difficulty? Why?

• Deepen, expand, and revise plans when evidence indicates that students are not succeeding.

• Deal with team issues that arise because of the dynamics of the team.

• Identify needed areas of organizational support (e.g., access to the computer lab, money for a field trip, extra time from the librarian).

To address these topics, Harriet scheduled team meetings; set the agenda; made sure that the hard copy curriculum unit was brought to the meetings; invited others as needed; and gathered data about student performance through observations in the classroom, interviews, and collection of student work.

Harriet encountered three challenges in keeping the team healthy and productive. First, once in the throes of implementation, team members naturally experience frustrations, unresolved

---

FIGURE 6.3
Mini-Case Study of Skillful Facilitation

Mary-Pat, the facilitator, dealt with a difficult situation during the summer's curriculum design institute. The teachers were having a serious and impassioned conversation about their personal expectations for students. Mary-Pat recalled later that she could "smell" trouble brewing. But since the heated discussion occurred at the end of the day, she decided to "wait and see" what would happen the next day.

The next morning the situation spiraled downward. Just before lunch, Mary-Pat intervened to help the team process their problem. She began by asking the team to identify the problem specifically. Two women, both leaders in their own right, dominated the conversation with their opposing viewpoints. Everyone else remained silent. In essence, the problem was that one teacher wanted to use the I-Search Unit as a vehicle to accomplish the science fair, an annual event with a long tradition. The second teacher was vehemently opposed, saying, "I am not a science teacher. I am an English teacher. I am *not* doing a unit that leads toward science as an end." During the week, this teacher had been a dominating force; no one was brave enough to oppose her. The first teacher was a strong, assertive person, though not as domineering. After listening to the two viewpoints, Mary-Pat tried to elicit responses from the other team members, especially to clarify the district's expectations for the science fair. The second teacher was becoming more aggressive and more defensive, threatening to just drop out of the project. Since it was time for lunch, the meeting disbanded. Mary-Pat suggested that she and the second teacher have lunch together.

Alone with the teacher, Mary-Pat acknowledged that the teacher had the option to remove herself from the team, because participating was voluntary. However, Mary-Pat said she hoped that this would not be her choice since she seemed to have strengths to contribute and cared about the students. After a while, Mary-Pat found an excuse to leave. She headed for the principal's office to give him an update and to ask for help. He provided information on the science fair, supported Mary-Pat's strategies thus far, and offered to join the team if needed or wanted.

After lunch, tensions heightened. The two leaders continued their heated discussion, vehemently expressing their opinions. Mary-Pat shared information from the principal about the science project, but teachers asked questions Mary-Pat could not answer. Accepting his earlier offer, Mary-Pat invited the principal to join the meeting. When he arrived, the two sides stated their views. The group asked for clarification from the principal. Members were ultimately surprised when he said they need not do something "just because they had always done it in a particular way before." They could make their own decisions, apart from "downtown" or the principal.

This unexpected power and authority seemed to diffuse the team's anger. They proceeded to agree on a compromise. Rather than making the decision about the science fair project right then and there, they would present the question to all teachers in the school in the fall. Then, everyone would have the opportunity to vote on what would be best for the school and the students.

issues, and tensions between individuals. Harriet helped the team identify and resolve these issues. The second challenge was accountability. Harriet wanted to help her teachers better understand the direct link between teaching and learning. The third challenge, closely related to the previous one, was to keep pushing teachers to assess student performance against a set of criteria. After the unit ended, Harriet guided the team to prepare for their retreat by helping them to pose questions and gather data. At the retreat, she helped them analyze data and articulate recommendations.

Another important role Harriet served was that of a liaison, traveling back and forth between the teachers and the school administrators to make arrangements, get approvals, set up meetings to discuss issues, and gather materials and resources. This leads us directly to looking at how administrators can be supportive.

Involving Administrators for Support

We know from the literature and our own experience that reform around curriculum, instruction, and assessment cannot take place without the support of district- and school-level administrators. From the beginning, the superintendent, principals, and other key administrative personnel need to understand what is involved in an inquiry-based, I-Search Unit, and the implications for organizational support.

For example, if teachers are working as an interdisciplinary team, they need a structure for working together, must share a common group of students, must have common planning time, and need to develop a set of shared goals. Putting these prerequisites in place may necessitate changes in scheduling, including time for planning and longer blocks of time for sustained student work. Once teams are in place and ready to focus on curriculum, instruction, and assessment, other issues often arise. For example, teams might want greater access to computers, the library, and instructional materials. Many teachers might need more support from technology specialists, librarians, and media specialists.

Also, a typical outgrowth of inquiry-based instruction is that report cards can come under scrutiny as teachers realize they want the grading system to reflect new forms of authentic assessment. Budgetary issues can also arise (e.g., How to pay for release time so that teachers can meet during school? How to finance teachers' summer work? Where to find money to purchase supplies? How to pay for external facilitators?).

In Lowell, Francene Donahue had a strong commitment from the superintendent and from her supervisor, Peter Stamas. Besides offering financial support, both administrators were able to articulate to the principals and other school leaders the importance of supporting the innovation. Peter was particularly vocal in explaining the district's responsibility to every child and how change at the curriculum level could benefit all students, including those in general education, bilingual education, and special education. He provided both inspiration and ground-level support. In turn, at the school level, principals made sure that teachers had sufficient time to meet by finding hidden pockets of time in the school day, reshuffling schedules, and even taking over classes in a pinch (Zorfass & Donahue, 1997).

To maintain open lines of communication among administrators and teachers, the facilitator schedules meetings on a regular basis. The agenda often includes items like these:

- How do we tighten our links to standards?
- Can we adjust the curriculum to make time for this project?
- Do we need to take a closer look at grading and reports now that we are into inquiry?
- How do we keep track of what students are learning?
- Is there money to purchase needed materials for the library?
- How can we find money for field trips?
- What help can we have to inform parents about our new unit and solicit their support?
- How can we free up the librarian and media specialists to help teachers?

These questions are not answered once and then forgotten. They need renewed attention and discussion as new aspects of the questions come to light. Many schools create site-based management teams to address issues like these in a proactive way.

Final Comments

As the famous logo of the "swoosh"™ appears on the TV screen, the voice-over in the commercial for the well-known sneaker manufacturer intones, "Just do it!" This follows on the heels of video footage showing a perspiring athlete who successfully pursued his or her own life's dream. The message is a strong one, "Find your own 'it'!" "Lift yourself up!" "Get going!" Borrowing from the business world, what if the "it" we were

disseminating were the I-Search Unit rather than a product we were marketing? What footage would we use to create a compelling incentive? What would motivate middle school educators to "just do it!"? We'd be smart advertisers if we relied on three messages: Just do it because it benefits students; just do it because it raises teachers' professionalism; and just do it because it furthers middle school reform. Here are some ideas for our "advertisement."

- *Just do it because it benefits students.* Marion Wright Edelman stated in a magazine interview, "We don't have a child to waste" (Terry, 1993, p. 5). Although at the time she was talking about early childhood programs, her sentiment aptly applies to young adolescents in middle schools. If, through the I-Search, we can encourage 10–14-year-olds to *believe that they can learn*, if we give them the tools in the unit that they need for learning; and if we provide the support they need so they *do learn*, then they have an early start on being successful as future students, employees, and members of their families and communities.

- *Just do it because it raises teachers' professionalism.* Engaging in a cycle of curriculum design, implementation, and evaluation can revitalize teachers. They find that they have landed on the other side of an innovation not only intact, but stronger for having taken the leap. They have a broader repertoire of classroom-based teaching skills and a deeper appreciation of their own ability as teachers. The following comment expresses the sentiments of a teacher who took a risk with the I-Search, worked hard at implementation, and reaped the reward:

I recall one defining moment. My class was in the media center. I was surrounded by students, all investigating different questions. Anxiety gripped me. As "the teacher," I had never before been in a position where I didn't know all the answers. As I shook off my fear, I found that I could ask students the kinds of questions that helped them to take ownership of their learning. I realized I wasn't relinquishing control. Instead, I was helping my students take control of their learning.

• *Just do it because it furthers middle school reform.* There is a chasm in the middle school reform movement. On one side is the desire for interdisciplinary teams of teachers to collaborate around good, strong curriculum. On the other side are teachers, still working in isolation, unable to make the connection to each other and to a developmentally appropriate and rigorous curriculum (Ames & Miller, 1994). The I-Search Unit, as a catalyst for change, can begin to fill this chasm. George and Shewey (1994) characterize middle schools as a "work in progress." The I-Search seeks to accelerate that progress by opening the door to inquiry-based instruction, active learning, student-centered curriculum, and a constructivist approach to developing deep understanding.

Finally, Cuban (1997) asserts that teachers and administrators act as gatekeepers who admit or block change in schools. The I-Search Unit can be the key to helping the gatekeepers unlock the gates, allowing everyone associated with the middle school (e.g., students, practitioners, support staff, and families) to enter the realm of inquiry and active research.

Appendix
Planning and Assessment Criteria

A-1. Criteria for Phase I Immersion Activities

- Does the activity introduce, define, or elaborate one or more of the overarching concepts of the theme?
- Does it elicit prior knowledge and build knowledge?
- Is the activity developmentally appropriate?
- Does it allow time for processing?
- Does it model a method of gathering information by *reading, watching, asking,* or *doing?*
- Is the activity linked to one or more desired student outcomes?
- Are ways to assess students built into the activity?
- Will the activity intrigue students and provoke them to pose questions?

A-2. Criteria for Students' I-Search Question

- It relates to the theme and overarching concepts.
- It reveals the student's passionate interest.
- It is researchable by gathering information from varied resources and materials.

A-3. Guidelines for Student Peer Conferences

- *Students.* Which students would make the best peer conferencing partners? What factors should be considered to create balance (e.g., I-Search question, verbal ability, cognitive level, gender, communication style)?
- *Content.* What should be the focus of the conversation? How much structure should be placed on the conversation before it begins?
- *Conversational supports.* What will help students to be respectful listeners and effective conversationalists?
- *Materials.* What should students bring with them to the conversation to make it concrete (e.g., notes, portfolios, journals)?
- *Follow-up.* What follow-up in terms of notes will be expected?

A-4. Contents of I-Search Paper

- My Search Question (What was my question? Why did I care about this? What did I already know as I started my search?)

• My Search Plan (What is the story of my search? What materials and resources did I use? What helped or hindered my work? How did I overcome problems?)

• What Information Did I Learn as a Result of My Search? (What are the important ideas? How do these ideas link to one another in a meaningful way? What information or evidence supports these ideas?)

• What This Content Means to Me (What conclusions can I draw? What interpretations can I make? What next questions interest me?)

• What I Have Learned About Myself as a Researcher (What can I now do that will help me be a researcher in the future? What are my next goals?)

• References

• Appendixes

A-5. Specific Criteria for a Written or Multimedia Report

My Question

• Have a strong lead or good opening. Draw the reader into the topic with a good lead. For example, a story, quote, questions, startling statement.

• State your research question as clearly as possible. Show how it relates to the theme and overarching concepts of the unit.

• Explain your personal interest or connection with the question. Why did you care about the question?

• Tell what you already knew about the topic when you began the search.

The Search Process

• Describe the sequence of steps you followed in your search—what sources you started with and what other sources these led you to.

• Describe the materials and resources you used. Which were the best sources of information? Why?

• Describe any problems you encountered in locating information and how you solved them.

• Explain how the questions changed, expanded, or were revised over time.

• Share any breakthroughs: Tell when it really got interesting.

• Tell about how people contributed to helping you do your search.

What I Learned

• Provide basic information to set the context.

• Present three or four major findings, conclusions or big ideas. In doing so, integrate information from your various sources. Support these main ideas with examples, details, stories, and arguments.

• Connect this information with the original question.

• Show the products of any analysis you have done. Present tables, charts, graphs, timelines, maps, etc., that helped you make sense of information. Explain your analysis and draw conclusions.

What This Means to Me

• Explain how your knowledge has grown since your starting point.

• Explain what you learned that means the most to you, and explain why this is significant.

• Explain how this knowledge will affect what you think, believe, and know.

• Present any conclusions, recommendations, predictions, etc.

• Present next questions that you would be interested in exploring.

How I Have Grown as a Researcher

• Explain how you developed as a researcher: what skills or abilities did you develop.

• Tell how you appreciate yourself as a researcher, writer, presenter.

• Comment on what things you did well and the things that were difficult.

• Set some new goals for inquiry.

• Identify ways in which you helped or were helped by classmates and teachers.

• Talk about what you would change or do differently if you were doing another I-Search unit.

References

• Provide all references in alphabetical order.

• Use the correct format.

Appendixes

• Identify and letter each appendix.

A-6. Sample Rubrics for Each Section of I-Search Paper

Rubric for Evaluating I-Search Paper: Section: My Search Question

Criterion	4	3	2	1
Strong Lead	Arouses reader interest; draws reader into the topic using a captivating lead	Awareness of audience; uses some enticing ways to engage audience	Provides matter-of-fact introduction; little awareness of audience	No lead
Question Stated	Question is clearly stated and makes strong link to overarching concepts as appropriate	Question is clearly stated; mention is made of overarching concepts, but link is tenuous	Question is poorly stated; weak link to overarching concepts	No question and/or no connection to overarching concepts
Personal Connection	Detailed explanation of why question is motivating	Some explanation of why question is motivating	Unclear explanation of personal connection	No explanation of personal connection
Starting Point	Detailed description of starting point	Some information provided	Unclear or sketchy information provided	No description of starting point

Scoring Note: A score of 4 is excellent; 3, good; 2, fair; 1, poor.

Rubric for Evaluating I-Search Paper: Section: My Search Process

Criterion	4	3	2	1
Sequence of Steps	Provides complete and detailed sequence of steps of search	Provides description of key steps in sequence	Describes key steps, but not presented in sequence	No list of steps provided
Materials and Resources	Provides clear and complete description of materials and resources used	Lists key materials and resources used	Lists a few of the materials and resources used	No materials or resources are listed
Problems	Fully describes the problems encountered in locating information and the ways in which they were solved	Gives a brief overview of problems and solutions	Briefly mentions the problems encountered but does not explain solutions	No description of problems encountered
Change/ Revise Question	Provides clear and complete explanation of changes and revisions to question and provides rationale	Gives a brief explanation of changes and revisions and a brief explanation of rationale	Briefly describes changes and revisions; no explanation provided	No mention made of changing or revising question
Breakthroughs	Fully describes breakthroughs, clearly explaining what was interesting and exciting	Describes any key breakthroughs; gives highlights of what was interesting and exciting	Briefly mentions breakthroughs, no details provided about what was interesting and/or exciting	No description of breakthroughs offered
Helpers and Collaborators	Names all helpers and collaborators provided with clear explanation of their role	Names provided for key collaborators and helpers; offers brief explanation of their role	Names some helpers and collaborators; no mention made of their role	No mention made of help or collaboration

Scoring Note: A score of 4 is excellent; 3, good; 2, fair; 1, poor.

Rubric for Evaluating I-Search Paper: Section: What I Learned

Criterion	4	3	2	1
Sets Context	Provides relevant information to introduce and set a clear context for the major findings	Sets the context by providing basic information	Briefly mentions the context, without elaboration	Provides no context
Major Findings	Clearly presents all major findings in a well-organized way with supporting information and details	Provides key findings; information organized in a logical way; supporting details included	Presents a few findings, not well organized; few supporting details	Does not present findings
Connects to Questions	Provides a detailed explanation of how the information was gathered and how it is related to the I-Search question	Logical explanation given about how information links to I-Search question	Loose link given between information and I-Search question	Does not connect findings to I-Search question
Presents Analysis	Presents relevant analyses—tables, charts, graphs, timelines, maps, etc.; provides clear and meaningful explanations, interpretations, and conclusions	Presents relevant analyses; some explanation, interpretation, and conclusions provided	Provides analyses; no explanations, interpretations, or conclusions provided	Does not provide products of analysis

Scoring Note: A score of 4 is excellent; 3, good; 2, fair; 1, poor.

Rubric for Evaluating I-Search Paper: Section: What This Means to Me

Criterion	4	3	2	1
Self-Assessment	Provides a clear and detailed explanation of how knowledge has grown since beginning of search	Provides overview of how knowledge has grown since beginning of the search	Provides little information about knowledge growth since the beginning of the search	No self-assessment provided
Significance	Provides a full and clear explanation of why this information is significant, providing examples	Provides some explanation about significance	Provides scanty explanation about significance	No explanation of why information is significant
Impact	Provides a full and clear explanation of what impact this information will have on thinking, beliefs, and actions	Provides some explanation of impact on thinking, beliefs, and actions	Provides very brief explanation of impact on thinking, beliefs, and actions	No explanation of impact
Interpretation	Presents conclusions, recommendations, and predictions, fully explaining reasoning	Presents some conclusions, recommendations, and predictions, supported with some explanation	Presents very brief conclusions, recommendations, and predictions; no explanation of reasoning	No conclusions, recommendations, or predictions provided
Next Question	Presents a thoughtful set of next research questions and provides a clear explanation of motivation and rationale	Presents next research questions and provides an explanation of motivation and rationale	Briefly presents next research questions; no explanation or elaboration provided	No next research questions are provided

Scoring Note: A score of 4 is excellent; 3, good; 2, fair; 1, poor.

Rubric For Evaluating I-Search Paper: Section: Growth as a Researcher

Criterion	4	3	2	1
New Skills and Abilities	Provides a clear and detailed explanation of how research skills and abilities have grown during the unit; provides examples	Provides an explanation of how research skills and abilities have grown; provides some details and examples	Provides brief explanation of how research skills and abilities have grown	No explanation provided
Self-Assessment	Provides a clear and detailed explanation of what was done well and what were the problem areas; provides examples	Provides a clear explanation of what was done well and what the problem areas were	Provides a very brief explanation of what was done well and what the problem areas were	No self-assessment provided
New Goals	Clearly defines and sets new goals for acquiring research skills and abilities; explains reasoning	Sets selected goals for acquiring research skills and abilities; provides why this is important	Sets one or two goals for acquiring research skills and abilities; provides no rationale	Sets no goals
Help and Collaboration	Provides a clear and detailed explanation of ways in which help and collaboration were given and received; gives examples, explains impact	Provides a clear explanation of ways in which help and collaboration were given and received; gives at least one example, briefly mentions impact	Briefly explains ways in which help and collaboration were given and received	Provides no explanation
Application	Fully explains what about the search process would be done the same or differently in subsequent search	Provides good explanation of what would be done the same or differently in subsequent search	Briefly explains what would be done the same or differently in subsequent search	Provides no explanation

Scoring Note: A score of 4 is excellent; 3, good; 2, fair; 1, poor.

Rubric for Evaluating I-Search Paper: Section: **References**

Criterion	4	3	2	1
Alphabetized	All references are alphabetized	Occasional errors in alphabetization	Few references listed alphabetically	References are not alphabetical
Format	Correct format used throughout (as determined by teachers)	Close approximation to correct format	Format is not followed correctly	Incorrect format used

Scoring Note: A score of 4 is excellent; 3, good; 2, fair; 1, poor.

Rubric for Evaluating I-Search Paper: Section: **Appendixes**

Criterion	4	3	2	1
Identified and Lettered	Each appendix is identified and lettered; corresponds to text	Most appendixes are identified and lettered; most correspond to text	Few appendixes are identified and lettered; few correspond to text	No appendixes

Scoring Note: A score of 4 is excellent; 3, good; 2, fair; 1, poor.

A-7. Criteria for Ongoing Student Self-Assessment

- *Completeness.* Each part of the overall report or exhibition is complete. It does not contain irrelevant information,
- *Creativity.* Students demonstrate imagination and originality. They use available resources and tools to creatively convey information.
- *Style.* The author's style is appropriate to the medium and to the purpose of the writing. The work reflects its author's distinctive use of language.
- *Media.* A variety of media are appropriately incorporated in a coherent and meaningful way.
- *Affect.* The author conveys passion, enthusiasm, pride of accomplishment, and a desire to help others learn.
- *Convention and mechanics.* Students use correct usage, whatever the medium.

A-8. Curriculum Development Process

1. Refine Theme and Identify Overarching Concepts

2. Identify Desired Student Outcomes Linked to Standards

3. Design Phase I Activities

- Brainstorm and evaluate activities.
- Plan calendar.
- Write description of each activity, including assessment.

4. Design Phase II Activities

- Determine criteria for *read, watch, ask,* and *do.*

5. Design Phase III Activities

- Schedule library and media center.
- Design minilessons to teach strategies for meaning making.

6. Design Phase IV Activities

- Determine criteria for I-Search paper; generate rubrics.
- Determine criteria for exhibition; generate rubrics.
- Determine plan for drafting, revising, editing, and publishing.

7. Develop Building Block Activities

- Journals
- Portfolios
- Bulletin Boards
- Paper Outline
- Exhibition Guidelines

8. Next Steps

- Review plan.
- Make up "to do" list.
- Assemble curriculum.
- Plan for further meetings.

A-9. Table of Contents for I-Search Curriculum Unit

1. Theme and Overarching Concepts
2. Student Objectives

3. Four Phases of the I-Search Process

4. Phase I

- Goals
- Calendar
- Activity Planning Guides
- Criteria for a Good Question

5. Phase II

- Goals
- Calendar
- Decisions
- Activity Planning Guides

6. Phase III

- Goals
- Calendar
- Activity Planning Guides
- Assessment Criteria

7. Phase IV

- Goals
- Calendar
- Activity Planning Guides
- Report Outline
- Assessment Criteria Report and Exhibition
- Plans for Dissemination

8. To Do List

A-10. Evaluating the I-Search Unit Implementation

- What factors facilitated or hindered implementation of the unit?
- What was the effect of the unit on the students, on each one of us as professionals, and on the team as a whole?
- In what ways could we improve, expand, or deepen the unit in the future?
- Based on our experience, what advice would we give other teams just starting out?

References

Ames, N., & Miller, E. (1994). *Changing middle schools: How to make schools work for young adolescents.* San Francisco: Jossey-Bass.

Beane, J. (1990). *A middle school curriculum: From rhetoric to reality.* Columbus, OH: National Middle School Association.

Brooks, J. G., & Brooks, M. G. (1993). *The case for constructivist classrooms.* Alexandria, VA: ASCD.

Brown, A., & Campione, J. (1996). Guided discovery in a community of learners. In K. McGilly (Ed.), *Classroom lessons: Integrating cognitive theory and classroom practice* (pp. 229–270). Cambridge: The Massachusetts Institute of Technology Press.

Caine, R. N., & Caine, G. (1991). *Making connections: Teaching and the human brain.* Alexandria, VA: ASCD.

Caine, R. N., & Caine, G. (1997). *Education on the edge of possibility.* Alexandria, VA: ASCD.

Carrigg, F., & Ramella, G. (1996, September). It's the curriculum, stupid. *Electronic Learning, 16*(1), 56–57..

Cohen, J. (1971). *Thinking.* Chicago: Rand McNally.

Cuban, L. (1997, January 27). *Implementation of research-designed innovations.* Keynote address at the Meeting of the Technology, Educational Media, and Materials Cross Project, Washington, DC.

Gardner, H. (1983). *Frames of mind: The theory of multiple intelligences.* New York: Basic Books.

Gardner, H. (1993). *Multiple intelligences: The theory in practice.* New York: Basic Books.

George, P. S., & Shewey, K. (1994). *New evidence for the middle school.* Columbus, OH: National Middle School Association.

Gilligan, C. (1990). Preface: Teaching Shakespeare's sister: Notes from the underground of female adolescence. In C. Gilligan, N. P. Lyons, & T. J. Hanmer (Eds.), *Making connections: The relational worlds of adolescent girls at Emma Willard School* (pp. 6–29). Cambridge, MA: Harvard University Press.

Harmin, M. (1994). *Inspiring active learning: A handbook for teachers.* Alexandria, VA: ASCD.

Herman, J. L., Aschbacher, P. R., & Winters, L. (1992). *A practical guide to alternative assessment.* Alexandria, VA: ASCD.

Howard, C. (1993). *Team collaboration: Let's make it work for students.* Unpublished manuscript.

How Children Learn. (1997, March). *Educational Leadership, 54*(6, Whole Issue).

Hyerle, D. (1996). *Visual tools for constructing knowledge.* Alexandria, VA: ASCD.

Inspiration [software]. (1992). Portland, OR: Inspiration Software, Inc.

Jacobs, H. H. (Ed.). (1989). *Interdisciplinary curriculum: Design and implementation.* Alexandria, VA: ASCD.

Jacobs, H. H. (1997). *Mapping the big picture: Integrating curriculum and assessment K–12.* Alexandria, VA: ASCD.

Joyce, M. Z., & Tallman, J. I. (1997). *Making the writing and research connection with the I-Search Process.* New York: Neal-Schuman Publishers, Inc.

Kaszyca, M., & Krueger, A. M. (1994). Collaborative voices: Reflections on the I-Search Project. *English Journal 83*(1), 62–65.

Lang, G. (Ed.). (1995). *Educational programs that work: The catalogue of the National Diffusion Network.* Longmont, CO: Sopris West.

Lawrence, D. H. (1988). Whales weep not. In R. Ellmann & R. O'Clair (Eds.), *Norton anthology of modern poetry* (2nd ed.). New York: Norton.

Macrorie, K. (1988). *The I-Search paper.* Portsmouth, NH: Boynton/Cook.

Manning, M. L. (1993). *Developmentally appropriate middle level schools.* Wheaton, MD: Association for Childhood Education International.

Marzano, R. J., Pickering, D., & McTighe, J. (1993). *Assessing student outcomes: Performance assessment using the Dimensions of Learning model.* Alexandria, VA: ASCD.

McDonald, J., Barton, E., Smith, S., Turner, D., & Finney, M. (1993). *Graduation by exhibition: Assessing genuine achievement.* Alexandria, VA: ASCD.

McDonald, J. (1992). *Three pictures of an exhibition:*

Warm, cool and hard. (Studies on Exhibitions, No. 1). Providence, RI: Coalition of Essential Schools, Brown University.

Morocco, C., & Nelson, A. (1990). *Writers at work: A process approach to writing for grades 4 through 6.* Chicago: SRA, Macmillan/McGraw-Hill.

Morocco, C., & Zorfass, J. (1996). Unpacking scaffolding: Supporting students with disabilities in literacy development. In M. C. Pugach & C. L. Warger (Eds.), *Curriculum trends, special education, and reform* (pp. 164–178). New York: Teachers College Press.

National Council for the Social Studies. (1994). *Curriculum standards for social studies: Expectations of excellence.* Washington, DC: Author.

National Council of Teachers of English and International Reading Association. (1996). *Standards for the English language arts.* Urbana, IL/Newark, DE: Authors.

National Council of Teachers of Mathematics. (1991). *Professional standards for teaching mathematics.* Reston, VA: Author.

National Research Council. (1996). *National science education standards.* Washington, DC: National Academy Press.

Orrell, C. J. (1996). ATLAS communities: Authentic teaching, learning, and assessment for all students. In S. Stringfield, S. Ross, & L. Smith (Eds.), *Bold plans for school restructuring* (pp. 53–74). Mahwah, NJ: Lawrence Erlbaum.

Parsons, L. (1990). *Response journals.* Portsmouth, NH: Heinemann.

Perkins, D., & Blythe, T. (1994). Putting understanding up front. *Educational Leadership, 51*(5), 4–7.

Pool, C. R. (1997). Maximizing learning: A conversation with Renate Nummela Caine. *Educational Leadership, 54*(6), 11–15.

Presseisen, B. Z. (1985). Thinking skills: Meanings, models, materials. In A. Costa (Ed.), *Developing minds: A resource book for teaching thinking* (pp. 43–48). Alexandria, VA: ASCD.

Progoff, I. (1980). *The practice of process meditation.* New York: Dialogue House Library.

Schmoker, M. (1996). *Results: The key to continuous school improvement.* Alexandria, VA: ASCD.

Search Organizer [software]. (1996). Newton, MA: Education Development Center, Inc.

Sizer, T. (1992). *Horace's school. Redesigning the American high school.* New York: Houghton Mifflin.

Slavin, R. E. (1990). *Cooperative learning: Theory,* research, and practice. Englewood Cliffs, NJ: Prentice-Hall.

Smith, C. (1995). Integrated language arts. In J. O'Neil (Ed.), *ASCD curriculum handbook* (pp. 3.19–3.31). Alexandria, VA: ASCD.

Sternberg, R., & Williams, W. (1996). *How to develop student creativity.* Alexandria, VA: ASCD.

Sylwester, R. (1995). *A celebration of neurons: An educator's guide to the human brain.* Alexandria, VA: ASCD.

Terry, W. (1993, February 14). We don't have a child to waste: An interview with Marion Wright Edelman. *Parade Magazine,* 2–5.

Timeliner [software]. (1994). Watertown, MA: Tom Snyder Productions.

Urdan, T., Klein, S., Medrich, E. (1997). *Early adolescence: A review of the literature.* Washington, DC: U.S. Department of Education, Office of Educational Research and Improvement.

Vygotsky, L. S. (1978). *Mind in society: The development of higher psychological processes.* (J. Cole, V. John-Steiner, S. Scribner, & E. Souberman, Eds. and Trans.). Cambridge, MA: Harvard University Press.

Wittrock, M. C. (1986). Students' thought processes. In M.C. Wittrock (Ed.), *Handbook of research on teaching* (3rd ed.). New York: Macmillan Press.

Zahorik, J. A. (1997). Encouraging—and challenging—students' understandings. *Educational Leadership, 54*(6), 30–32.

Zemelman, S., Daniels, H., & Hyde, A. (1993) *Best practices: New standards and learning in America's schools.* Portsmouth, NH: Heinemann.

Zorfass, J. (1991). *Make it happen! Inquiry and technology in the middle school curriculum.* Newton, MA: Education Development Center, Inc.

Zorfass, J. (1996). *Make it happen! Inquiry and technology in the middle school curriculum* (rev. ed.). Newton, MA: Education Development Center, Inc.

Zorfass, J., & Copel, H. (1995). The I-Search: Guiding students toward relevant research. *Educational Leadership, 53*(1), 48–51.

Zorfass, J., & Donahue, J. F. (1997). *Initiating, sustaining, and expanding a middle school initiative* [On-line]. Available: http://www.edc.org/FSC/MIH/

Zorfass, J. M., Morocco, C. C., & Lory, N. (1991). A school-based approach to technology integration. In J. O'Neil (Ed.), *ASCD curriculum handbook* (pp. 11.51–11.95). Alexandria, VA: ASCD.

About the Authors

Judith M. Zorfass is an Associate Center Director at Education Development Center, Inc. She has worked in middle schools across the United States since 1986 as an educational researcher, a curriculum developer, a staff developer, and a trainer-of-trainers. She is the lead developer of the Make It Happen! approach which guides teachers to design, implement, and evaluate I-Search Units. She also oversaw the development of the *Search Organizer* software, which supports students through the I-Search process.

Zorfass's career in education has spanned more than 30 years. During that time, she has taught children with and without disabilities (including students with learning disabilities and students who are deaf), has worked in the publishing business, and has been an educational researcher at EDC for many projects funded by the U.S. Department of Education. She is a frequent presenter at national conferences and a contributor to journals. She received her doctorate from the Reading and Language Department at the Graduate School of Education at Harvard University.

Harriet Copel is principal of the Howard B. Mattlin Middle School in Plainview-Old Bethpage Central School District, New York. She has also worked in Lawrence, New York, first as District Coordinator of Instructional Technology and then as Assistant Principal in Lawrence Middle School. At the middle school, she oversaw the implementation on I-Search Units by teams of 7th grade teachers. She has also traveled to numerous school districts to guide interdisciplinary teams to develop I-Search Units.

Over the past 25 years, Copel has served as a special education teacher, a classroom teacher, a learning disabilities specialist, and the coordinator of microcomputers in a regional special education agency. She presents frequently at regional and national conferences. She holds a master's degree from Columbia Teachers College and a professional diploma from Long Island University.

Address correspondence to the authors as follows:

Judith M. Zorfass, Associate Center Director, Education Development Center, Inc., 55 Chapel Street, Newton, MA 02158-1060 (e-mail: JudyZ@edc.org).

Harriet Copel, Principal, Howard B. Mattlin Middle School, Plainview-Old Bethpage Central School District, 100 Washington Avenue, Plainview, NY 11803 (e-mail: HCopel@aol.com).